# LIGHTING THE WAY

A LITTLE MAGIC BOOK OF SPIRITUAL MESSAGES AND MEANINGS

By Eileen McCourt

# Lighting The Way

## By Eileen McCourt

This book was first published in Great Britain in paperback during April 2021.

The moral right of Eileen McCourt is to be identified as the author of this work and has been asserted by her in accordance with the Copyright, Designs and Patents Act of 1988.

All rights are reserved and no part of this book may be produced or utilized in any format, or by any means, electronic or mechanical, including photocopying, recording or by any information storage or retrieval system, without prior permission in writing from the publishers - Coast & Country/Ads2life. ads2life@btinternet.com

**All rights reserved.**

**ISBN: 979-8732045963**

**Copyright © April 2021 Eileen McCourt**

# CONTENTS

Messages and meanings:

1. My soul will go on
2. We are the God Essence
3. How we are
4. I am eternal consciousness, infinite awareness
5. God is the All
6. I am unconditional love
7. There are no mistakes
8. There are no accidents or chance happenings
9. Energy and how it works
10. No judgement in Spirit
11. Forgiving and being forgiven
12. Just be!
13. We are co-creators
14. God has no form
15. Protecting yourself
16. So you think you are free?
17. Meaning of the word 'individual'.
18. As above, so below
19. Living in alignment
20. Uniqueness and diversity in Oneness
21. Earth's problems are spiritual
22. You are the script-writer and director in your own stage production
23. It's all about the soul

24. It's how you deal with what happens that is important

25. Only light can drive away the darkness

26. Consciousness

27. I go on forever

28. Christ Consciousness

29. Veil of forgetfulness

30 Reality

31. Raising your energy vibration

32. Getting connected

33. Being true to yourself

34. A time of no-time -  the cosmic hologram

35. Eternity

36. There is no death

37. Religion versus spirituality

38. The Higher Self

39. What happens when I pray?

40. Meditation

41. Energy, vibration, frequency , - those 3 words!

42. Mother Nature, - teacher, guide, nurse, provider

43. Karma

44. God is not to blame!

45. Ego

46. The man in the mirror

47. The colours of the rainbow

48. Everything flows in a natural rhythm

49. Creating a new world, - we need tools, not weapons

50. Creating ripples -  casting pebbles

51. Crystal, rainbow and star children
52. Unconditional love
53. Trust in the universe
54. There is no such thing as an absolute of anything
55. There is no right or wrong way, just different ways
56. Healing
57. Everything is in order
58. The universe is a mirror
59. The hero within each of us
60. Life's but a game!
61. The truth will always be revealed
62. Where intention goes, energy flows
63. I create my own soul song
64. It's all about the journey
65. Be like the eagle
66. Cause and effect
67. My soul knows where to go
68. Everything has both a masculine and a feminine element
69. Everything is vibration
70. Everything comes from the same Source
71. Everything originates in in the One Great Universal Mind
72. The 3-plumed flame of love, knowledge and power
73. A Sioux Indian prayer
74. This great awakening
75. Man's greatest challenge
76. It's awonderful world
77. Native Indian 10 commandments

78. Follow your heart

79. The here and now

80. Gratitude

81. Responsibility

82. Choosing your crystals

83. Living with joy

84. Giving and receiving

85. Music of the Spheres

86. The earth is a living organism

87. Living from your heart

88. Your body is a beautiful manifestation of  Father/Mother God

89. We are only passing through

90. Ho'Oponopono

91. We are not alone in the universe

92. You have the power

93. Our hope for the future

94. The meaning of Namaste

95.  I AM

96. Atonement -   At-One-Ment

97. Know thyself

98. Happiness is..........

99. De-clutter!

100. Let your Light shine!

# ABOUT THE AUTHOR

Eileen McCourt is a retired school teacher of English and History with a Master's degree in History from University College Dublin.

She is also a Reiki Grand Master teacher and practitioner, having qualified in Ireland, England and Spain, and has introduced many of the newer modalities of Reiki healing energy into Ireland for the first time, from Spain and England. Eileen has qualified in England through the Lynda Bourne School of Enlightenment, and in Spain through the Spanish Federation of Reiki with Alessandra Rossin, Bienstar, Santa Eulalia, Ibiza.

Regular workshops and healing sessions are held in Elysium Wellness, Newry, County Down; New Moon Holistics N.I. Carrickfergus, County Antrim; Angel Times Limerick; Holistic Harmony Omagh, County Tyrone; Spirit 3, Ballinasloe, County Galway; Celtic School of Sound Healing, Swords, County Dublin; Kingdom Holistic Hub, Mill Road, Killorglin County Kerry, and Reiki Healing Bettystown, where Eileen teaches all of the following to both practitioner and teacher levels:

- **Tibetan Usui Reiki levels 1, 2, 3 (Inner Master) 4 (teacher) and Grand Master**
- **Tera-Mai Reiki Seichem**
- **Okuna Reiki (Atlantean and Lemurian)**
- **Reiki Karuna (Indian)**
- **Rahanni Celestial Healing**
- **Fire Spirit Reiki (Christ Consciousness and Holy Spirit)**
- **Mother Mary Reiki**
- **Mary Magdalene Reiki**

- Archangels Reiki

- Archangel Ascended Master Reiki

- Reiki Seraphim

- Violet Flame Reiki

- Lemurian Crystal Reiki

- Golden Eagle Reiki  (Native North American Indian)

- Golden Chalice Reiki

- Golden Rainbow Ray Reiki

- Goddesses of Light Reiki

- Unicorn Reiki

- Pegasus Reiki

- Elementals Reiki

- Dragon Reiki

- Dolphin Reiki

- Pyramid of Goddess Isis Reiki

- Kundalini Reiki

- Magnified Healing of the God Most High of the Universe

- Psychic Surgery

- Merkaba Activation and Meditation

Details of all of these modalities can be found on Eileen's website, together with dates and venues of courses and workshops.

This is Eileen's **33rd** book.
Previous publications include:

- *'Living the Magic'*, published in December 2014

- *'This Great Awakening'*, September 2015

- *'Spirit Calling! Are You Listening?'*, January 2016

- *'Working With Spirit: A World of Healing'*, January 2016

- *'Life's But A Game! Go With The Flow!'*, March 2016

- *'Rainbows, Angels and Unicorns!'*, April 2016

- *'........And That's The Gospel Truth!'*, September 2016

- *'The Almost Immaculate Deception! The Greatest Scam in History?'*, September 2016

- *'Are Ye Not Gods?' The true inner meanings of Jesus' teachings and messages'*, March 2017

- *'Jesus Lost and Found'*, July 2017

- *'Behind Every Great Man........ Mary Magdalene Twin Flame of Jesus'*, July 2017

- *'Out of the Mind and into the Heart: Our Spiritual Journey with Mary Magdalene'*, August 2017

- *'Divinely Designed: The Oneness of the Totality of ALL THAT IS'*, January 2018. Also in **Audiobook**, May 2019

- *'Resurrection or Resuscitation? What really happened in That Tomb?'*, May 2018

- *'Music of the Spheres: Connecting to the Great Universal Consciousness and to ALL THAT IS through the music of Irish composer /pianist Pat McCourt'*, June 2018

- 'Chakras, Crystals, Colours and Drew the Dragon: A child's second

**Spiritual book',** July 2018

- *'The Voice of a Master: It is Jesus Himself Who Speaks: Know Thyself',* December 2018

- *'Kundalini',* January 2019

- *'Brave Little Star Child Comes To Earth'* - Audiobook- April 2019

- *'The Truth will set you free. - Christianity: Where did it all begin?'* May 2019

- *'Titus Flavius Josephus: Did Josephus write the gospels?'* June 2019

- *'Homo SPACIENS: We Are Not From Planet Earth! Our connection with UFOs, ETs and Ancient Civilisations'* August 2019

- *'Those Strange Looking Men In Their Flying Machines: Visitors From Beyond Time and Space? Or From Planet Earth? ETs, UFOs and Who Knows What'* September 2019

- *'I Want to Break Free: Helping our Planet Earth ascend to a higher vibration of Love, Joy, Peace and Happiness for all. We can do it!'* November 2019

- *'The Universe is Mental! Understanding the 7 Spiritual Laws of the Universe, the Hermetic Principles that govern Creation'* January 2020

- *'To Be Or Not To Be.... The Man of Stratford who was never to be Shakespeare: Exposing the deception that was William Shakespeare'* February 2020

- *'If Not Shakespeare, Then Who? Unmasking the Real Bard of Avon! '* April 2020

- *'What On Earth Is Happening? 2020: Year of Balance: Rise of the Divine Feminine'* April 2020

- *'Creating a New World! - Nature WILL be obeyed! - The greatest lesson never taught, but which we need to learn'* May 2020

- *'Humanity's Greatest Challenge? Breaking out of the vortex of ignorance and superstition'* May 2020

- *'Puppets on a String! But! The Strings have been broken! We are free!'* July 2020

- **'Out of the Darkness of Deception and Despair - Into the Light of Truth'** February 2021

Podcasts for each of the 33 books can be viewed on Eileen's website and on her author page.

The recent series of weekly videos, *'Our Great Awakening',* together with the previous series *'The Nature Of.........'* with Eileen and Declan Quigley, Shamanic practitioner and teacher, can also be viewed on Eileen's website and on YouTube, together with a series of healing meditations and Shamanic journeys.

Eileen has also recorded 6 guided meditation CDs with her brother, composer/pianist Pat McCourt:

- *'Celestial Healing'*

- *'Celestial Presence'*

- *'Cleansing, energising and balancing the Chakras'*

- *'Ethereal Spirit' - Meditation on the 'I Am Presence'*

- *'Open the Door to Archangel Michael'*

- *'Healing with Archangel Raphael'*

Eileen's first DVD, *'Living the Magic'* features a live interview in which Eileen talks about matters Spiritual.

All publications are available from Amazon online and all publications and CDs are in Angel and Holistic centres around the country, as specified on website.

Please visit also the BLOG page on Eileen's website.

Website: www.celestialhealing8.co.uk

Author page: www.eileenmccourt.co.uk

YouTube channel:
https://www.youtube.com/channel/UChJPprUDn19Eeu01rRjGsqw

# ACKNOWLEDGEMENTS

Book number *33!*

And so for the *33rd* time, a sincere thank you, not just to my publishers, Don Hale O.B.E and Dr. Steve Green, but also to all the wonderful, amazing team I have around me! You all know who you are! And you all know I could not do any of this without each and every one of you! Those who are with me all the way, not just in getting the books published, but those who are involved in all the other necessary work that goes along with all that I do. And those of you who are constantly sharing my posts on Facebook, getting me to people whom I would never otherwise reach!

And of course, not forgetting all of you who are buying my books and CDs wherever you are, and all who have taken the time to give me feed-back, and to write reviews for me, both in my books and on Amazon. You are greatly appreciated.

Thank you to all who attend my courses, workshops and meditation sessions, sharing your amazing energies, taking us on such wonderful journeys and through such amazing experiences! We are all so blessed!

And thank you to all of you who have been following myself and Declan Quigley on Facebook in our present video series *'Our Great Awakening'*, and in our meditations and Shamanic journeys. We just hope they are bringing some comfort and help to you in these uncertain times in which we now find ourselves!

And as always, I give thanks for all the great blessings that are constantly being sent  our way in this wonderful, loving, abundant universe.

Namaste!

Eileen McCourt

3rd May 2021

# FOREWORD

The lighthouse beams its light out into the starry blackness of the night, penetrating the darkness, affording guidance and comfort not just to those at sea, but also to those on land. Its light continues to shine through, no matter what the weather, no matter what the conditions. Its rotating flash, - a beacon, a friendly, heart-warming signal that lights up the way. A welcoming light in the darkness of the night, a reassuring message that someone is looking out for us, keeping us safe.

Hence the title of this book, and the photos on the front and back covers. The spiritual messages are meant to bring positivity, comfort, reassurance, to guide us through the darkness, to show us the way.

This book is different from all my previous books in that it does not need to be read from beginning to end, from cover to cover. All the messages and their meanings are numbered 1-100, so just open at any page!

We need to keep the Light turned on! Only the Light can drive away the darkness!

I hope these spiritual messages will be a beacon of Light for you, as you continue on your own evolutionary soul path.

And I hope that you too will continue to be a lighthouse, beaming out your beautiful rays to all those who are searching for the Light. Your beautiful Light affording hope, support and rescue to those still trapped in the darkness.

May you always walk in the Light!

Namaste!

x

**1.** I am a spiritual being having a physical experience for the duration of this life time only. This physical body is not everything I am. It is only the transportation vehicle, the conduit, for my Soul on my journey through this life-time. I HAVE a body, but I AM a soul. My physical body, like an old coat which I no longer need, will be discarded at the end of this physical life-time. But my soul will go on, - on to the next stage of my soul evolutionary process, in another level of reality, on a different, a higher level of energy frequency, - a higher energy dimension than this lower third dimension energy level of this world.

**2.** To view humanity as being in the physical only, and to perceive the purpose of life as physical evolution only, is to miss out entirely on the meaning of who we really are, and the real purpose behind our physical, temporary embodiment and our temporary sojourn here on Planet Earth.

We are essentially, fundamentally and inherently God essence. That is our inherent nature! And claiming our God nature is not some form of spiritual arrogance, - it is simply acknowledging our own divine essence, our own divine nature, our own true being.

**3.** I am the God essence in physical form. I am only here because the God energy has manifested me. Like the wave in the ocean. Like the shapes in the fog.

The wave is in the ocean only because the ocean has thrown it up, the ocean has created it. The wave has no life outside of the ocean, it has no other place to ever be in existence except within the ocean. The wave builds up and then crashes. It is no longer a wave, but it is still within the ocean. Just in a different form.

Likewise, the shapes are in the fog only because the fog has formed them, the fog has thrown them up. They have no other place to be in existence except in the fog. The shapes ARE the fog. The shapes continuously merge and separate, merge and separate, merge and separate, each time taking on a different form.

That is how we are. We are ever only in existence because the Great God Energy has thrown us up, has created us, has formed us. Like the wave in the ocean, and like the shapes in the fog, we come and we go throughout all of eternity, changing form, but always within the One Great Universal Energy, the One Great Universal Consciousness, the One Great Universal Intelligence we call God. There is no other place for us ever to be in existence except within the One Great Universal Energy we call God.

**4**. I am eternal consciousness. I am infinite awareness. I come and I go. I go on for ever. Travelling through all the energy frequency dimensions throughout all of creation and throughout all of eternity. I am the Great God Energy experiencing itself in physical form. I am the Great God Energy in physical manifestation. I am the Great God Energy experiencing its own creativity. Like Shakespeare's characters. Shakespeare created those characters. They are only in existence because Shakespeare created them. They came from the mind of Shakespeare. Shakespeare is in them, and they are in Shakespeare. They are Shakespeare and Shakespeare is them. They are an extension, an aspect, a manifestation of his creativity. I am in God and God is in me. I am an aspect, a manifestation of God's creativity.

**5.** God is The All. God IS All. God is in everything and everything is in God. I am in God and God is in me. I am in everything and everything is in me.  I am the Light. I am the God Essence. I am the wind. I am the bird. I am every leaf on every tree.  I am every tiny grain of sand.  I am every beautiful raindrop. I am the flowing river. I am the rolling ocean. I am the rising and the setting sun. I am every delicate snowflake.

I AM!  I AM, - within the One Great Universal God Energy.

**6.** I am love. God is Love. There is only one kind of love and that is unconditional love. Saying '*I will love you if you do......* ' is not love. That is manipulation. That is controlling. Unconditional love is seeing myself, first of all, as the bright spiritual being I truly am, and then seeing everyone else as the bright spiritual beings we all are. And because I see myself as the bright spiritual being I truly am and everyone else as the bright spiritual beings we all are, then I do not criticise, I do not judge, I do not hate and I do not condemn or kill. I send out only pure unconditional love from my heart center, with no conditions attached.

Unconditional love does not mean that I see myself and everyone else through rose-coloured spectacles. No one of us is perfect. If we were, then we would not need to be here on this earth plane, on this earth energy dimension level. Unconditional love does not mean that I turn a blind eye, being in denial about the weaknesses or negative traits of another. Rather, unconditional love is acknowledging these negative traits, but at the same time seeing beyond them and still sending that person unconditional love. I know you have murdered someone, but I still visit you in prison. I know you have done the most horrific of deeds, but I see beyond those to the bright spiritual being you truly are. You are NOT those horrendous deeds you have done. You are simply, through those horrendous deeds, fulfilling your Soul contract for your journey through this life-time, whatever that may be. And I do not know what your Soul contracts are, or what your mission in this life-time is, and so I cannot judge. Just like the characters in the soap-operas or in a stage production, all of whom are simply fulfilling their contract to play out certain roles in any particular drama, so too each one of us is simply playing a stage-role, as part of our Soul contract.

Unconditional love is total acceptance of myself as I am here and now, and total acceptance of everyone else as they are, here and now. No judgement, no criticism, just total acceptance. And with no expectation of any return. Just knowing that we are all playing a particular role in the drama of life!

**7.** There is no such thing as making a mistake. Everything is a learning experience, a learning process. I am here on this earth plane for the purpose of soul expansion. This is the sole (!) reason why each and every one of us is here on this earth energy vibration level, why each and every one of us has freely and willingly chosen to re-incarnate time and time again, - to expand our soul, to evolve our soul, and so raise our spiritual consciousness and the spiritual consciousness of all humanity. And we can only achieve that through continually experiencing, experiencing, experiencing, and through experiencing as much as we possibly can experience, learning the lessons we have set out to learn in each life-time.

A baby starts to crawl. Then he begins the learning process of walking. He takes his first tentative, uncertain steps and then falls. But we don't ever think of saying '*Oh, you made a mistake. Start again!*' No! We know the child will learn to walk in his own way and in his own time, and not in our time. He will get the hang of it all when he is ready. And he will fall many times, over and over again. But he is not making a mistake of any kind. He is simply going through the learning process, - and all by experiencing! We all need to learn! And we learn through experiencing!

**8.** There is no such thing as an accident, luck, chance, or coincidence. There is only synchronicity. Nothing just *'happens'*. Synchronicity is simply the coming together in the universe at the right time of all the elements needed to manifest something or some event.

Everything and everyone in my life is here for a purpose. To help me learn and progress on my spiritual path. I need to look beyond the hurt anyone has caused me and find the lesson I am meant to learn from it. And when any relationship ends, I need to send that person forward with Love and Light and gratitude for having given me the opportunity to learn some particular lesson.

And if I do not learn that particular lesson, then it will keep presenting itself to me in some way, recurring time and time again in my life until I recognise that lesson and learn from it.

For example, many people, both male and female suffer abuse from their partner, - whether mental, emotional or physical. Then they leave that partner and find themselves with a new partner who does exactly the same to them. What has happenend here? The lesson needing to be learned here is the lesson of self-respect. Until that person recognises and learns *'I respect myself. I will never again allow anyone to disrespect me in this manner. I deserve only the best '*, they will continue to attract the same type of person into their lives, one who will continue the abuse pattern. And why? Because they are sending out the message *'I am not good enough. I have no respect for myself. I am not worthy'*.

When they change their thoughts and opinions about themselves, then they will begin to attract a different kind of person into their life.

**9.** I am energy. Everything and everyone is energy. And the only difference between us all is the rate at which our energy is vibrating.

The Angels and the Higher Beings of Light do not see me as I am in physical form. They have no eyes, or any of the five physical senses that I have. They resonate and identify with the rate at which my energy is vibrating. The more spiritually aware I am, then the faster my energy vibrates. And when I pass over after this physical life-time, the only way I will be identified will be by the rate at which my energy is vibrating, and my soul will automatically gravitate towards the energy frequency vibration level to which I have managed to get myself in this life-time.

Energy is changing all the time, it is in constant motion and movement. When we meet someone and fall in love, that is because the energy of both people is resonating and vibrating at the same rate, hence they are attracted to each other. But energy is always in a state of change. If two people change together and grow in the same direction, then that is wonderful and they will stay together. But that does not always happen. People change in different ways, they begin to grow apart, and this is when the harsh words, the fighting, the cruel accusations begin.

And how do you solve this? The only way forward is to accept that this relationship is now at an end, it has now run its full course. Then move on, thanking that person for the lessons they have taught you, and sending them not resentment or anger, but Love and Light.

**10.** There is no judgement in Spirit, - ever! There is no criticism, no condemnation, no punishment in Spirit, - ever! The only place you will ever experience judgement, criticism or punishment is in a physical life-time on this low density earth energy vibration level. And why is there no judgement, condemnation or criticism in Spirit? Simply because there is no need for any of that. And why not? Simply because the higher level energy frequencies that are Spirit do not indulge in or tolerate any of the lower energy frequency forms of negativity. And that's the reason why they are on a high vibration energy level, - because they are above and beyond all low-level energy stuff. Also, Karma takes care of everything. Karma negates the need for punishment. Karma is the internal safety mechanism built into our world. Karma is the balancing of our not-so-good deeds with our good needs, and no one of us escapes that balancing. What you send out in your thoughts, words and actions goes out on a certain energy vibration level and attracts more of the same back to you. So we all get back what we send out. We reap what we sow. As we treat others, so too will each one of us be treated. That's one of the Great Spiritual Laws of the Universe. Irrefutable! Indisputable! Inviolable!

**11.** We need to forgive and we need to be forgiven. When I am holding anger or resentment against either myself or against any other person, I am the one who is suffering. When I am not forgiving someone, when I am withholding forgiveness from someone who has hurt me, either by word or action, I am carrying a great weight around my neck. When we forgive, we release ourselves from this great burden. We are free!

Lack of forgiveness, bearing grudges, holding resentment are all negative low energy vibrations. And I cannot pass on to my next stage of existence if I am carrying any of these. Negative energy like this will hold me back on my spiritual evolution. I must forgive and rid myself of that negative heavy burden which I am carrying.

Likewise, I need to be forgiven. If I pass on to my next stage of existence and someone is still holding a grudge against me or still has not forgiven me for some hurt I have caused, then again, that negative energy will hold me back on my spiritual development. I must seek that person's forgiveness and put any wrongs to right.

**12.** Just be!  The universe knows exactly what you need and what you want!  And the universe does only one thing. The universe delivers! When we worry about the least little thing, what we are saying to the universe is '*I don't trust in you!*'

We all go after a particular type of person, a particular house, a particular job, a particular car, and we set out our own agenda, trying to move heaven and earth in our attempts to get what we want.

But the universe might not have that in mind for us! The universe has something else in store for us, something much better, something which will make us much more happy. And all we are doing in this pursuit of our own aims, in pursuit of our own agenda, is just interfering in the natural flow of cosmic energy which brings all good things to us. So what do we do?  We send out our request, yes of course we do. BUT!  We do not get attached to the outcome! Leave that to the universe. The universe has everything under control.

So we just need to '*just be!*' Yes, take the necessary steps, make the necessary arrangements, and then back off!  Hand it all over! Hand it all over to the universe! And the universe will deliver!  Because that is what the universe does!

**13.** We are all co-creators within the One Great Universal Energy we call God. This One Great Universal Energy, this One Great Universal Consciousness does only one thing. It creates!

Creation is constant, ongoing and eternal. Creation is the One Great God Energy experiencing itself through its own creativity. Creation is the One Great Universal God Energy expressing itself in diverse forms of life.

And we are all co-creators within that One Great Universal God Energy. That means we create. We create and sing our own Soul song. If we are boxed in by religious or other institutional teachings and dogmas, we are singing someone else's song, dancing to someone else's tune.

And we cannot co-create if we are singing someone else's song! Creativity is an expression of freedom. Each and every beautiful soul yearns to fly freely, to find expression in the glory of creation, flying freely between all the multitudinous energy frequency vibration levels that make up all of creation. Finding expression! Finding expression through its own magnificent power of creativity! Creating its own unique song, singing its own unique song, sounding its own unique note, contributing to the harmony of the One Great Universal and Cosmic Orchestra!

And how do we create? We create with our thoughts! Our thoughts create our reality.

And we have a great responsibility for the thoughts we send out! Simply because our every thought will manifest! We are in control of the type of world we create! All the thoughts we send out must come from higher levels of energy vibration frequency than the lower dense energy level of this earth plane. Hence, we must always be aware of the energy level on which we are operating. We must always keep our vibration level high!

**14.** God is not a being of any kind. God has no form, no matter, no mass, no physicality. God has no eyes, no ears, - none of the five physical senses we humans have, that connect us to the physical world around us.

There is only the One Great Universal Heartbeat. All is synchronised within this One Great Universal Heartbeat. There is only the One Great Universal Pulse. Everything pulsates and beats in rhythm with this One Great Universal Pulse. And there is only the One Great Universal Breath. All life is contained within this One Great Universal Breath. All forms of life are connected through this One Great Universal Breath. We are not just breathing in and out, - we are also **being breathed** in and out. We are all **part of** a much greater Intelligence, and not **apart from** this One Great Intelligence.

When you see the wave, you see the ocean. The wave **is** the ocean. When you see the shapes in the fog, you see the fog. The shapes **are** the fog.

And when we see ourselves, we see God. We are of the same substance. And not only are we **of** the same substance, - we **are** the same substance. We **are** the God Essence.

Everything is energy. God is energy*. 'Thee'* Great Universal Energy. Omnipresent, omniscient, omnipotent.

The Great One Universal Energy, the Great One Universal Consciousness, the Great One Universal Mind, - this is what we call God.

And this One Great Universal Energy we call God does only one thing, - it creates. It continues to find expression through its own creativity, continuously and eternally experiencing itself. Experiencing itself through us!

**15.** There is no such thing as a punishing God. The punishing God we have all been led to believe in does not exist. There is no such thing as punishment in Spirit. The only place where you will experience judgement or punishment is on this earth plane.

The universe has safety mechanisms built into it, built into all of life. One of these safety mechanisms is, - '**What I send out, I get back'.**

It's all about energy! Every thought, every word I send out goes out on a certain energy vibration frequency level. All energy attracts more of the same back to it. Low energy vibration attracts more low energy back to it. High energy vibration attracts more high energy vibration back to it. However, there is an anomaly here! Like attracts like, - yes! But high energy vibration frequency attracts not only the same back to it, but also lower vibration energy frequency, - energy vampires, all on the prowl for their '*fix', their* food, their energy boost!

And when you arrive home after your day, and you don't understand why you are feeling so exhausted, so lacking in energy, - well, that's because you have been depleted of energy! Sucked dry! The vampires have got you! They have had a feast!

And all because you have not been protected!

And how do you protect yourself? Very simply by drawing the White Light of Spirit around yourself first thing every morning and invoking the Blue Cloak of Archangel Michael to cover you completely. And not just in the morning! You need to top that all up throughout the day. We are constantly in contact with other levels of energy vibration frequency, and while some give us an instant lift, others pull us down to a lower vibration energy level. And these are the ones against whom we need protection.

Shopping centres are full of negative energy! Shop-keepers are on a mission to sell, sell, sell, desperate to make money. Shoppers are on a mission to buy, - for whatever reason! In many cases, - retail therapy! To cheer themselves up! To lift their spirit!

See all the negative energy at play here? So before you go anywhere, protect yourself!

**16.** So you think you are free? Really? In response to this question, most of us immediately think yes, we are free, - and we think of countries like Nazi Germany, Communist China or Russia, where we see life as being very different from our own.

But in how far are we actually free?

We spend our days working to pay a mortgage, to buy the necessities of life, to pay our taxes, - we are slaves to work! How can that be free?

We are bound in with laws, rules and regulations, whether from religious or other controlling institutions - we are told how to think, how to act! How can that be free?

We are even told how to dress, - we are slaves to fashion! How can that be free?

We are brainwashed by education systems, mainstream media, advertising, all sorts of political spin and propaganda. How can that be free?

And what is freedom?

Freedom is singing your own soul song, not singing someone else's song. Freedom is dancing to your own tune, not dancing to someone else's tune.

Freedom cannot be found in man-made laws! Simply because man-made laws, by their very nature, are controlling. Freedom can only be found in the great Spiritual Laws of the Universe.

Consider the analogy of the lion in the cage!

The lion in the cage, whether in a zoo, circus or safari park, is not free. He is trapped, tied in, subjugated, held in by whatever means, by those who wish to exploit him for their own mercenary ends, and not his benefit.

He appears to be well cared for. The conditions of his own natural habitat are re-created, - temperature, natural trees and grass, and he is fed raw meat several times each day. Yes, well looked after, one might say! Except! He is being deprived of the right of his own natural instincts. The lion's natural instincts are to roam the grasslands or prairies of Africa, and to hunt for his own food. Both of these he is being denied. He is singing someone else's song! He is dancing to someone else's tune! His soul is not flying freely to sing its own glorious song. He is not being allowed to contribute his own beautiful note to the glorious harmony of the great cosmic orchestra.

Now let us put ourselves in the place of that lion.

We are curtailed, hemmed in, restricted by all sorts of laws and impositions placed upon us by government, religious, education and other institutions, not to even mention societal thinking and restraints. We are slaves to constant work, simply to pay for our basic necessities, to pay the mortgage, to pay the bills. We are burdened with more and more taxation exactions.

And we think we are free? Far from it! We are controlled! Man-made laws, creeds, doctrines, institutions do not bring freedom! Simply because by their very nature, they are controlling! And the chief weapon being used against us in order to control us is fear! And what does fear do? Fear creates paralysis. Paralysis in mind and in body. Paralysis in society. Suffocation. And when people are suffocating, they will grasp at any straw!

And how do we guarantee real freedom for ourselves in this physical world? Freedom can only be achieved when we understand and live within the 7 Hermetic Principles, otherwise known as the 7 Great Spiritual Laws of the Universe. An understanding of, and an adherence to these laws is our passport to freedom, our manual for an abundant, fulfilling life. Freedom from all the man-made distortions, artificial creeds and doctrines that permeate our world. So, if we are to summarise what we need to know in order to lead a happy, fulfilled life, in order to experience real freedom, then we can summarise it all in just a few points:

- Energy - both masculine and feminine needs to be in balance

- Vibration - we are in control

- Ups and downs in life - energy is constantly changing, nothing lasts

- Living in the Oneness of the Great One Universal Mind

- Communication - which is constantly going on between all the multitudinous levels of energy frequency, and we must be open to receive

- Our thoughts create our reality. Each one of us is the master, not the victim. We are in control!

And to repeat! Freedom cannot come from any man-made laws, creeds or institutions, simply because they, by their very nature, are controlling mechanisms. Freedom can only come from your soul flying freely, singing its own unique soul song. Each of us has our own unique soul note. Each of us has our own unique soul song. We cannot sing anyone else's soul song! And no one else can sing ours.

Many of us, unfortunately, are singing someone else's song.

Take back your power! You ARE the power! Let your beautiful soul fly freely to sing its own glorious song, contributing its own glorious note to the glorious harmony of the One Great Cosmic Orchestra!

Sing your own Soul song!

That is real freedom!

**17.** What do we understand by the word '**Individual**'?

The word '**Individual**' actually comes from the Latin word '**Individus**', meaning **'one and indivisible'.** In other words, inseparable.

So we, as '**individuals**' are actually indivisible, inseparable.

Indivisible, inseparable from what or from whom?

Indivisible and inseparable from the One Great Universal Energy, the One Great Universal Consciousness we call God. And indivisible and inseparable from each other and from every other form of life!

We are not '**individual**' in the sense we have been led to believe. We are **NOT** separate beings, we are not separate from all other forms of life. We are not separate from Source, from '*All That Is*'. There is no '*I*' or '*me*', or '*you*'. There is only the collective '*we*'.

We are all part of the same chain of divine, universal energy that runs through all things, supporting all things, manifesting all things. We are all connected. There is no separateness.

All of creation, in its entire totality, is connected. It is this understanding of connectedness with '*All That Is*' that will enable us to reach a higher understanding of ourselves as consciousness and energy, constantly changing, but immortal, infinite, never-ending.

I am you and you are me. We are all One. We are all inseparably connected within the one great All That Is. What I do to another, I do to myself.

Chief Seattle, a prominent leader of the Duwamish Native Americans, in the State of Washington, and after whom Seattle was named, wrote:

*'Man did not weave the web of life, he is merely a strand in it. Whatever he does to the web, he does to himself'.*

And again:

*' All things share the same breath, - the beast, the tree, the man. The air shares its spirit with all the life it supports.'*

**18**. As above, so below.

Our Planet Earth is part of a solar system which is part of a galaxy, which is part of our universe, - '**uni-verse**', meaning all one. We are only one of twelve universes. All the planets in the entire Milky Way, in all the universes in the entire cosmos, with their diverse, inter-planetary forms of energy, are all connected with us here on Planet Earth. All our actions, deeds and thoughts affect each and every other aspect of this vitally connected, exquisite tapestry of life.

All the sky stuff, all the earth stuff, all forms of life, are all one big living mass of energy. There is consciousness in everything, in all that exists on earth, in all that exists in the universe, in all that exists in the entire cosmos. All consciousness communicates constantly and continuously on electro-magnetic frequencies, throughout all vibrational dimensions. These frequencies connect and have a universal and cosmic unified investment in working together for the benefit and highest good of all.

The problem with humanity is that we believe we are separate from all this universality and cosmically combined flow of energy. Our current mistaken belief that we are separate and our current mistaken understanding of the word '*individual*', is a barrier to us seeing, accepting and therefore accessing, the wholeness and entirety of existence. All we are doing is disempowering ourselves even further, cutting ourselves off from the very same Source that we need for our own existence. Like the leaf on the tree. The leaf does not exist as a separate entity. The leaf does not exist just on its own. It is part of the branch, which in turn stems from the trunk, which in turn gets its life force from the earth.

Our earthly bodies respond directly to whatever is happening anywhere else in this entire, vast network of creation, as we sense it all through our cosmic umbilical cord.

We have highly sensitive, internal mechanisms which work in tandem with all that is happening in all the other areas as well as in our Planet Earth. The weather systems, for example! The effect they have on our physical bodies! We often complain about feeling '*under the weather*'. Many of our physical ailments are a direct result of the weather. Our respiratory rate, our blood circulation, our heart beat, our fluid circulation, - all are affected by the weather patterns. And the firmaments affect even our mental state! Especially our mental state! The word '*lunar*', as in pertaining to the moon, is encapsulated in the word '*lunatic*', the moon having a great pull on our minds, and of course, on the tides of the oceans, preventing the huge expanses of water from swallowing up our land masses.  Humidity affects our health, as do temperatures, altitude, wind direction and wind strength. Whenever the earth's magnetic field is disturbed, there is always a correspondingly adverse re-action in human physiology and psychology.

Ancient and medieval peoples knew and understood the connectedness between what was happening on the earth plane and in the higher forces and dimensions in the rest of the entire cosmos.

So, yes, we are indeed multi-dimensional beings in a multi-dimensional universe, inter-relating, inter-connected on every level. The more we evolve, the more we grow in awareness and spiritual consciousness, then the more we will realise, understand and accept that there is a greater connectedness in the universe and in all things. The less evolved a person is, the less spiritually aware, the less spiritually open, the more engrossed and entrapped a person is in the physical body and the five physical senses, then the more that person will continue to perceive himself and everything else in his life as isolated, unconnected and separate.

**19.** When we live in harmony with our surroundings, we enjoy a sense of calm and tranquility. If, for example, you love the sea, then if you are living in an area far from the sea, or in a forested area, or even inland in the countryside, your body will not be in harmony, and you will not be in a healthy state of being. You will not be resonating with, nor will you be in harmony with the synchronised forces that mould and form each one of us. You will not be living in a matching vibratory rate with your geographical area. Matching vibratory rates create harmony; mismatching vibratory rates create disharmony and a discontentment within the mind and spirit, creating a general restlessness, the cause of which is very often beyond our immediate understanding.

Even the colours with which we choose to surround ourselves bring us contentment and tranquility if they match the vibratory rate of our aura; disharmony if they do not.

Everything has got to be in perfect alignment; all vibratory rates have got to match if we are to live in a healthy condition. Colour, scent, and sound vibrations are especially poignant sign-posts for us as to the state of our health. We all have natural elements that best harmonise with each one of us and if we are to be happy in our life, we must acknowledge and honour our inner promptings to follow the vibratory rates that best resonate with us.

**20.** We are all One. But there is still uniqueness and diversity in Oneness. We are all the same substance, all the same thing, all the same stuff, in an unbroken cycle, all in the one enormous infinite something, all an inherent part of the same one undivided whole, part of a continuum. Each one of us is a microcosm of the macrocosm that is all of creation. Each one of us is a tiny version of the One Great Universal Energy, the One Great Universal Consciousness we call God.

At the same time, each one of us is a unique expression of that One Great Universal God Energy. Unique and at the same time indivisible from the collective whole. It is indeed meaningless to view any one of us as a separate entity, as everything in creation is in a continuing and changing flow of energy.

Like the waves in the ocean. No two waves are similar, yet they are all contained within the ocean. They form as waves, build up to the crest, then break. They are no longer waves, but they are always remaining within the ocean. As waves, they move of their own volition, coming and going as waves all within the entirety of the ocean.

Like the leaves on the tree. Each leaf is unique in itself, yet at the same time all the leaves belong on the branch. Each branch is unique in itself. Each branch is connected to the trunk, which in turn gets its life-force from the earth.

Every living thing is unique and diverse in itself, but at then same time, every living thing is part of the greater whole. Part of the Oneness. Uniqueness and diversity in Oneness!

**21.** The problems here on our earth right now are neither political **nor** economic. The problem is actually a spiritual problem. And only a spiritual solution can be applied to solve a spiritual problem.

Unfortunately for humanity here on this earth dimension, we have been programmed to believe that this world is a competitive, individualistic place, where only the fittest survive. We have been imprisoned in this individualistic mentality for aeons and aeons of time, where we have looked with envy, greed and resentment on anyone who has more than we have, in the belief that we are seen and judged by others by the amount of worldly possessions we manage to accrue, the amount of money we can make, the numbers of letters we can get after our name. Believing in our own minds that we are competing individuals has made us into the egotistical, capricious, envious creatures we have become, instilling into us a mistaken compartmentalised view of the world in which we live.

We put up barriers between ourselves and others; we build walls of protection around ourselves; we hide our true selves behind facades and masks. In this individualistic thinking frame, we fail to get to know our neighbours. What we fail to know becomes strange. And what becomes strange to us becomes fearful to us. We harbour negative thoughts of insecurity, suspicion and envy. The green-eyed monster! The product of our individualistic way of thinking! Our greatly mistaken way of thinking!

So you see, the  problem with us here on Planet earth is a spiritual problem!  And only a spiritual solution can successfully be applied to solve that problem!

We are each other. We are the collective psyche. We are the

collective human mind. We are all One. I am you and you are me. What I do to anyone else, I also do to myself. If one person hurts, I too hurt. If we can rid the world of the false notion that it is every man for himself and that we are all separate, then there would be no envy, no greed, and above all, - no fear!

And if we could just start to see ourselves and everyone else as the beautiful spiritual beings each and every one of really is, then we are applying a spiritual solution! Simply because when we start to see each other in this light, then we will no longer criticise, we will no longer judge, we will no longer hate, and we will no longer kill.

And if we could just start to see that each of us is here, on this stage of life, to play a particular part, a particular role, to fulfill certain contracts made at soul level, then we would see beyond the physical body of each person, without judgement or condemnation.

And when we manage to get ourselves to this stage, then we are applying a spiritual solution, - the only way to solve a spiritual problem!

**22.** Each one of us has been here many times before, and each one of us will be here many more times again. Each one of our incarnations is only a miniscule part of all the roles we will play in our progress towards enlightenment, towards totality, towards completedness. We are here on this earth school to learn lessons. Lessons which will raise our own spiritual consciousness and the spiritual consciousness of all humanity. We serve two masters: our own spiritual evolution and the collective spiritual evolution of all humanity. As a species, we are, and always have been, advancing towards a common destiny, - that of total enlightenment.

You yourself and you alone, wrote the script for your own life. You yourself and you alone, freely chose the lessons you wish to learn this time around. You yourself and you alone, have freely chosen the time and the place, the lineage and the blood-line into which you would become embodied, into which you would be born, in order to provide the opportunities that would best serve your spiritual development here on Planet Earth.

You are the script-writer, you are the producer, you are the main player on the world stage, in the performance of the story of your own life!

**23.** Everything, absolutely everything we do and everything we experience is all about the Soul, all about Soul expansion. That is the sole(!) reason for us being here on this earth energy vibration frequency level.

Everything that happens to us, and every person who comes into our life is a direct result of the energy vibrations we ourselves have sent out.

There are just 3 words we need to understand in order to get our heads around all of this. And those 3 words? Energy, vibration and frequency. Everything is energy, vibrating at a particular frequency rate.

Put simply, we draw back to ourselves according to the energy vibrations we send out through our thoughts, words and deeds.

**24**. It is not what happens to us in life that is most important. What is most important is how we deal with what happens to us.

Each one of us is in control of how we react to any person, event or experience in our life.

For example, - say I offend you by a personal insult. I have the power to send out that insult, if I so choose. But I do not have the power to determine how you react. Only you yourself can decide that!

And you have 3 choices:

1.  You can let the insult, the hurt, really get to you. But what have you just done here? You have allowed me, you have handed over your power to me, to bring you down to a lower vibration energy level,  through the hurt you are now feeling.

2.  You can insult me back. But now have you just done?  Again, you have allowed me, you have handed over your power to me, to drag you down to my low energy vibration level. And I must be on a lower energy vibration level if I am insulting anyone.

3.  You can rise above it all. You can realise and accept that I must be on a lower energy vibration level, and you do not allow me to drag you down to my lower energy level. Instead, you send me Love and Light, as only Love and Light will raise my energy vibration to a higher level again. An eye for an eye and a tooth for a tooth only makes everyone blind and toothless!

So be like the eagle!  Soar above it all, seeing the whole picture.

No problem can be dealt with positively if we remain on the same energy vibration frequency level as that on which the problem has manifested in the first place. War cannot be met with more war. We cannot respond to violence with more violence. We must raise our consciousness level higher and view the whole situation objectively from our higher vantage point.

*'Getting even'? 'Getting revenge'?* We can only do that by lowering our energy vibration level.

And who in their right mind would want to do that?

In the words of Martin Luther King:

*'Returning violence for violence multiplies violence, adding deeper darkness to a night already devoid of stars. Darkness cannot drive out darkness; only light can do that. Hate cannot drive out hate; only love can do that'.*

**25.** Only light can drive away the darkness. When you go into a dark room, how do you get rid of the darkness? You do not scoop it all up and take it away in a bag! You turn on the light!  The darkness has not gone away anywhere, it is still there, - it has just been transmuted into the light. And when you turn the light off again, the darkness will return.

You never tell anyone to go into a room and turn off the darkness. Rather, you always tell them to turn on the light!  It is always the light that we turn on and off. Never the darkness.

The light is much more powerful than the darkness!  And if we keep the light turned on, the darkness cannot seep through.

**26.** What is consciousness?

Consciousness is a state of Awareness. Every form of life, no matter how tiny or how insignificant it may appear to be in its tiny being, has a certain degree of consciousness, a certain level of awareness inherent in its very state of existence.

And total Consciousness? Total consciousness is full Enlightenment.

Total Consciousness is Oneness. Enlightenment is Oneness. And we progress upwards through all the higher states and levels of consciousness towards a state of total consciousness, full Enlightenment, Oneness, as we become more aware of ourselves as spiritual beings, spiritual nomads, inter-dimensional, inter-galactic travellers, journeying through the vastness of eternity, beyond time and space.

What we see as the universe, in all its vastness, is not just a single physical world, but a mere fragment of a much greater whole. And that much greater whole, in which absolutely everything is contained and to which everything is permanently connected, exists without any beginning or end, in the here and now, in this present moment of what we call time. There is no such thing as the past or the future. There is only the present. And there is no other time zone for us to ever be, except in the here and now.

Time is not measured by the number of years we clock up. Time is measured by the rate at which we increase our level of spiritual consciousness, our level of spiritual awareness, our becoming aware of all the other dimensions of consciousness and energy vibration frequency levels in the entirety of creation.

And we are all destined to travel through all the multitudinous levels of consciousness on our eternal journey of soul expansion.

Many civilisations are light years ahead of us on the path to total awareness. Compared to them we are just babies. Our Planet Earth is amongst the youngest of civilisations in the entirety of creation, very obvious from the way in which we treat each other, with all the wars, killings, hatred, greed, envy, and all the other lower energy vibrations that are so much part of our earthly lives. We cannot even imagine what the technology, for example, of civilisations millions of light years ahead of us in consciousness or awareness levels, would look like, never mind what it can actually do! Those civilisations so far ahead of us in awareness and consciousness have powers that to us appear super-natural.  Those civilisations use their advanced knowledge and technology to help each other. And for what do we use ours? To kill each other! We as a civilisation have not yet graduated from our very primitive state of spiritual consciousness, we have not yet gained admission to the higher realities.

We are all in the process of growth. And the key to growth?

In the words of Lao Tzu, sixth century  B.C.E. Chinese philosopher, credited with founding the philosophical system of Taoism:

*'The key to growth is the introduction of higher dimensions of consciousness into our awareness'.*

**27.** I am eternal consciousness, I am infinite awareness. I have no end. I go on forever. Each one of us is an expression of infinite awareness, an infinite expression of consciousness, an unending stream of consciousness, having an eternity of experiences, and this life-time is just one of those experiences.

We are inter-galactic, inter-dimensional travellers, cosmic nomads, spiritual beings, travelling beyond time and space, into the endless depth and breadth of infinity and eternity, through all the different energy vibration frequency levels, traversing all the multi-dimensions that make up the entirety of creation. Creation is an on-going eternal process. That means it never ends. It is both infinite and eternal. Endless! There will always be new realities for us to explore. The Great Universal God Consciousness is a continuous, self-promulgating, self-expanding, self-generating energy. Always creating. Always expanding. So there is always something new for us to explore. And as inter-galactic, inter-dimensional travellers, it is our mission to explore all the other levels of reality, a process in a constant state of ongoing expansion, and hence with no end. We never catch up with ongoing creation.

I am eternal consciousness, I am infinite awareness. I have no end. I go on forever!

**28**. What is Christ Consciousness?

Christian; Christianity; Roman Christian Church; Christmas. - These are all words pertaining to and associated with the word '*Christ*'. And the word Christ to most of us means '*Jesus Christ',* as in the gospels.

The word Christ comes from '*Christos*', meaning the '*Anointed One*'. Many of the ancient gods were known as Christ, for example, the Egyptian Sun God Horus; the Greek God Dionysius, and the Roman-Persian God Mithra. So Jesus Christ, the God of Christianity was just the latest in a long line of gods known as '*The Christ*'.

So Christ is not a name. Jesus was not Mr. Christ. Christ is a title. A title that many of the ancient gods claimed!

The term '*Jesus Christ'* was first brought into being at the Council of Nicea, 325 C.E. by the Roman Emperor Constantine. The Council of Nicea was convened in order to cement together all the diverse cultures throughout the vast sprawling Roman Empire, and to create some sort of cohesiveness and unity. The '*Jesus'* part appealed to the followers of the new Roman Christian Church, and the '*Christ'* part appealed to others with their beliefs in the early religions based on the ancient gods.

Christ is a consciousness, a vibration, an energy frequency. It is on the vibration of love, and right at the very top of all the energy levels on that vibration. There are many and various types of love. For example, the love you have for your parents is not the same as the love you have for your spouse, or for your pet. Yes, it is all love, and no one type of love is any greater than any other. They are all just different, just varying degrees of the same thing.

Christ Consciousness is unconditional love. God is unconditional love. And the story in the gospels of the birth of Jesus at Christmas is symbolic of the birth of unconditional love within each and every one of us.

And what is our understanding of unconditional love? Unconditional love is seeing myself, first of all, as the bright spiritual being I really am, and seeing everyone else as the bright spiritual beings we all are. And because I see myself and everyone else in this way, I do not judge, I do not criticise, I do not condemn, I do not hate. I accept myself and everyone else exactly as we all are, negative behaviour patterns and all included. I see beyond the physical body to the bright spiritual being, here in physical embodiment, in order to fulfil soul contracts, all in pursuit of soul expansion.

And Christianity, as in Roman Christian Church, has been misrepresented to us, like many other aspects of religion.

The Roman Christian Church claims to be based on the teachings of Jesus in the gospels. Really? Those teachings were advocating love, acceptance, tolerance, forgiveness, compassion. A far cry from the history of the Roman Christian Church! It is a sad fact that no church, government or state has ever, in the entire history of humanity, based its practices on the teachings of Jesus in the gospels. And least of all that Church by the same name, - the Roman Christian Church! No single institution, in the entire history of humanity has caused more wars or suffering, has inflicted more violence, torture, killing, than the Roman Christian Church.

The Roman Christian Church is merely a business! But an extremely lucrative business! The wealthiest institution in the world! The Roman

Christian Church invented the big business of sin, and then proceeded to brainwash and lure its unsuspecting, trusting members into buying, for example, indulgences, and all sorts of other promises which would get one into heaven. Not forgetting of course, the great reward one could claim on arrival at the pearly gates if one had bequeathed land or estates to the church!

Recent television documentaries about Rome and the Eternal City have exposed the Roman Christian Church, the Roman Catholic Church for what it really is, - flamboyant, decadent, corrupt, manipulative, - all in pursuit of its lust for wealth and power. The extravagance, the opulence of the Vatican buildings, - all the decorative massive achievements and works of art of the likes of Michelangelo, such as the Sistine Chapel, - all meant to be a statement of power, dominance, supremacy, indestructability.

So make no mistake! Christianity as in Roman Christian Church, has merely used the word Christ  for its own devious ends. It has nothing to do with The Christ Consciousness, the energy vibration of unconditional love.

Each one of us, on our soul evolutionary journey, is progressing toward that highest of energy vibration frequency levels, within the whole One Universal Energy we call God. And then we too will earn the title *'Christ'*.

**29.** We have been here many times before, we have had many previous lives, all in pursuit of soul expansion.

Yet, why, when we are born into this earth energy vibration level, is there a veil of forgetfulness pulled down over our eyes? Why are we not allowed to remember our previous lives? Surely remembering what we have already achieved would help us?

The answer is, - no, remembering all of our past lives would only hinder us! How?

Well, firstly, we tend to re-incarnate in groups. So supposing you were to remember that your present partner was your mother, father, son or daughter in a previous life, then would that not interfere and affect your present relationship?

Secondly, and this is the hardest part for us to get our human minds around! There is no such thing as time in Spirit. There is no such thing as the past, all is in the present. Everything is happening in this present moment. But on a different level of reality. So that means that all those 'past' lives, all those 'previous' lives we think we may have had, are not in the past, they are not over and done with, they are not ended. They are happening right here and now! We are all experiencing simultaneous lives in the here and now! We are experiencing life in various levels of reality all at once! So we are not allowed to remember or to know about our 'other' lives, our 'other' personae, simply because we would be intruding! That person that is actually 'me' in another life-stream, in another existence, has his or her own stream of consciousness. And this is how we are all multi-dimensional beings. We are living multiple lives, not in a linear fashion, but at once, concurrently, simultaneously. We are existing in

53

many life-streams, all at once, all here and now, on many vibration energy frequencies. And that is what we mean when we say we are inter-galactic, inter-dimensional travellers! We are experiencing many different frequency energy levels, - all at once, all in pursuit of soul expansion.

Those who have had a near-death experience all testify to the feeling of complete Oneness, and to knowing everything and being aware of everything on differing levels of consciousness all happening at the same time, all happening currently, yet outside and beyond what we call our normal earthly dimension time flow, with no demarcations of space or time. A sort of inter-galactic, inter-dimensional, inter-cosmic, in-the-one moment event! According to Max Tegmark, one of the most original physicists at work today, and his theory of the multiverse and parallel universes, everything is everywhere and can be in existence simultaneously. The future, as well as the past, is here and now. All is in the now.

## 30. What is reality?

Reality is simply consciousness manifesting on various energy vibration levels, in different energy dimensions, on varying frequency energy realms. And reality for us, what we call reality, or reality as we know it or understand it to be, is simply a level of consciousness or awareness manifesting as we see it and experience it here in our physical world around us.

But this is not the only level of reality! This consciousness level on which we exist, on which we are experiencing what for us is reality, is not the only level of consciousness or awareness. There are countless other levels of consciousness, of awareness, multitudinous levels of reality all around us and interacting with us on a constant basis, and all operating on various frequency energy vibration levels. And their reality is not our reality for us at this point in earthly time. We cannot see or hear other reality levels because we are not tuned into their energy frequency level. The higher our own energy frequency level, then the easier it is for us to tune into those higher levels of reality. Animals are pure energy, as are young babies, as yet uncontaminated by the ways of this world, so they hear and see beyond this level of reality, - seeing and hearing what we as adults fail to see and hear.

When we are in our highest state of energy vibration, our energy is connected to, and aligned in harmony with the natural energy flow of the Universe. And being in this natural energy flow, in this alignment, enables us to tune into higher levels of consciousness, higher levels of reality beyond the reality of this physical world.

And just because we cannot see or hear all these other various and multitudinous levels of reality with our limited physical senses, that does not mean that they are not there! They are all around us, just on different energy frequencies.

Just like the channels on your television or radio. You cannot access any channel until you tune into it! And when you are tuned into one particular channel, the other channels have not gone away anywhere. They are all around you in the network, - you are just not tuned into them. The ship, as it goes beyond the horizon, is no longer in our vision. But it has not disappeared! It has just gone beyond our human vision. Likewise, the plane as it takes off, goes beyond our human vision. But it is still there!

So it is with all these different levels of reality all surrounding us. Just because we cannot see them with our limited human vision, does not mean they are not there. It simply means we have no access to them because our vibration is lower than theirs.

And that explains why we cannot see the higher Beings of Light, or even our dead ancestors. Simply because they are in existence on a different level of reality! But they are still there! All around us!

And the only difference between them and us is the rate at which our energy is vibrating! They are vibrating at a much faster rate than we humans are, - so fast that our human eyes cannot see them.

It is like looking into your washing machine. When it is spinning, it is going so fast that you cannot make out any particular item of clothing. But when it slows down you can see everything. Or like the propellor of a plane. When it is rotating rapidly, you cannot make out the separate blades. But when it slows down, then you can see the blades.

So we can only see what is on the same level of reality as we ourselves are. Raise your vibration, - increase your ability to connect with the higher Beings of Light!

**31.** How do we raise our energy vibration? We raise our energy vibration level by harbouring only high vibration energy level thoughts. Love, tolerance, compassion, caring, understanding, forgiveness, desire to help, non-judgement, non-condemnation, - these are all high vibration frequencies.

Conversely, - hatred, spite, greed, envy, desire for revenge, criticism, judgement, condemnation, - these are all low energy vibration frequencies.

And we have the freedom of choice as to whether we harbour low energy frequencies or high energy frequencies.

But remember! What you send out in your thoughts you get back, multiplied! That is one of the inviolable spiritual laws of the universe!

And to raise our energy vibration level, we also need to keep our physical body free from lower energy negative patterns and behaviours. Drugs, smoking, unhealthy eating habits, lack of sleep, lack of physical exercise, - these all keep our body trapped in the lower vibration energy levels. And eating meat is also keeping our body in the lower energy levels. And why? Simply because those animals whose flesh we eat, - they all die in trauma, and we are soaking that trauma into our digestive system. Even fish die in trauma, struggling for breath. Anything with a face should not be killed for food and eaten by us!

And finally, we raise our energy vibration by being connected to the One Great Universal flow of energy. Like the domestic appliances in our home, - they all need to be connected to the main electricity grid. Otherwise they just will not work!

**32.** How do we get connected? We need to be connected! Connected to what? Connected to the One Great Universal Energy we call God. Connected to Source! Just like the electric appliances or the plumbing works in our home. They all need to be connected to the mains!

And how do we know when we are connected? We are meant to be living in harmony. In harmony with other people and in harmony with our surroundings and Mother Nature. So we need to ask ourselves certain questions.

Am I happy in my life, in my relationships, in my marriage? If I have to think about it, if I hesitate at all in answering yes, I am happy, - then I am not happy! I am not connected to the great universal flow of energy, I am not connected to Source. So what do I need to do? I need to get myself out of that relationship and move on with my life!

Am I happy in my work? If I have to think about it, if I hesitate at all in answering yes, I am happy, - then I am not happy! I am not connected to the great universal flow of energy, I am not connected to Source. So what do I need to do? I need to get myself out of my present work into working at something I will enjoy!

Am I happy in my living conditions? Happy in where I live? If I have to think about it, if I hesitate at all in answering yes, I am happy, - then I am not happy! I am not connected to the great universal flow of energy, I am not connected to Source. So what do I need to do? I need to move to live where I will be happy!

Being connected is all about being happy. And whatever area of our life is causing us stress or pain or disharmony, then we need to change that! And when we change, then other doors will open for us. But we have got to make the first move!

We cannot live our lives in order to please anyone else or for the sake of anyone else. And we cannot force our children to follow in our footsteps in their career. They have their own life mission to follow, their own soul contracts to fulfill, their own lessons to learn. Their lessons are not our lessons, their soul contracts are not our soul contracts. And they have a right to follow their own path! To follow their own heart! If your son wants to cover his body in tatoos, get himself pierced in all sorts of places, grow his hair down to his ankles, and take off around the world with a guitar, then he has the right to do that. You may not like it, but there is nothing you can do about it! And doing nothing is always the hardest thing to do when you find yourself in such circumstances. But that is exactly what you must do! Nothing! It's his life, and he has the right to live it as he so chooses. You have your own life to be getting on with, and that should be enough for you!

Forcing or imposing your dictates on your children cannot be for anyone's benefit. Say for example, you force your children to take on the family business. If they are not happy going to work every morning, not enthusiastic about it all, only going to please their parents, then what kind of negative energy are they bringing to their work place? They will not be happy! Not happy because they are not connected! Not connected to Source! Not flowing in the great universal energy.

They will make their own connection to Source in their own way. And their way is not your way!

**33.** Being true to yourself.  In Shakespeare's famous play *'Hamlet'*, Polonius advises Laertes:

*'To thine own self be true, and it must follow as the night the day, thou canst not then be false to any man.'*

So what does being true to yourself mean?

Being true to yourself means doing what you enjoy doing and enjoying everything you are doing.

Being true to yourself means following your own natural talents and instincts, and not allowing anyone else to force you to follow a path they have chosen for you to follow.

Being true to yourself means pleasing yourself, not in a self-centered or selfish way, but in spending your life as you wish to spend it, because you know that is what you want, and you are not just trying to please others or keep others happy.

Being true to yourself means having fun and enjoying life, because that is what we are all meant to do.

Being true to yourself means acknowledging your own feelings. Very often we are told, *'Big boys don't cry!'* or *'Don't be such a cry-baby!'* But crying is natural for everybody, - girls, boys, men, women, babies. We are all composed of both a feminine side and a masculine side, and we have to let our feelings express themselves in the way we want to express them, and not hold them in, just in order to please anyone else.

Being true to yourself is being truthful about your own sexuality and about how you feel in your own body. If someone rejects you because of your sexuality, that is their problem, not yours. You have every right to express your own sexuality as you so wish.

When you go against your own natural instincts, living a lie, not being true to yourself, you are not doing anybody any favours, least of all yourself.

Always look for the good reason to do anything. And that will turn any negativity you may feel into positivity. For example, you have been asked to baby-sit tonight for someone, and you are not happy about it. So how do you be true to yourself, and yet at the same time not disappoint that person who has asked you to baby-sit? Remember, you cannot change anyone else's energy!  You can only change your own!

So very simply, - you think positively! This baby-sitting job you are doing is giving pleasure to someone else!  This baby-sitting job you are doing is perhaps buying you time to catch up on your reading! This baby-sitting job you are doing is earning you some money! This baby-sitting job you are doing is saving you the money you would have spent in your other plans for the evening!

So you see! You are being true to yourself! You have changed the whole situation around to please yourself!

Be happy! Be true to yourself!

So go on!  Dare to be happy!

**34**. Time, as we know it to be, as a demarcation factor, exists only on this earth energy vibration level. There is no such thing as time in Spirit, on the higher energy vibration levels.

Everything, absolutely everything that is, that ever has been, and that ever will be, is all happening at the same time, in the here and now! All happening in a timeless, no-time bubble! And how can this be explained? The explanation is in the cosmic hologram.

A hologram is a three-dimensional image of a whole and complete object. Large holograms take the form of a ghostly three-dimensional moving figure, so eerily convincing that you can walk around it and view it from all angles. But if you try to touch it, your hand will just waft right through it, reflecting the lack of physical substance or matter.

And the entire cosmos is a holographic image. The cosmic hologram in all its infinite vastness is the container of all creation. The vast depository of the photographic imprints of all that is, all that ever has been and all that ever will be. The infinite data-bank holding all information about all that is, all that ever has been, and all that ever will be.

The hologram as God. God as unconditional love. The hologram as love. The hologram as all of creation. Everything is contained within the Oneness of the hologram, within the Oneness of the Great Universal Energy, the Oneness of the Great Universal Consciousness, outside of which nothing and no person can possibly have any sort of existence. There is no other place, no other way of existing. Everything is within the hologram.

And the remarkable thing about a hologram is, that if we cut the holographic image up into tiny pieces, all of the holographic image continues to be contained in  each tiny piece. So every tiny piece is contained within the whole and the whole is contained within each tiny piece. Each tiny piece is a microcosm of the macrocosm, but at the same time, contains all of the macrocosm within it.

And it is the same with each and every one of us. Each one of us is a microcosm of the macrocosm that is all of creation. In other words, each one of us is just a smaller version of the One Great Universal Consciousness we call God. Each and every one of us is contained within the One Great God Energy, and that God Energy is contained within each and every one of us. Each and every one of us contains everything else and everything else contains each and every one of us.

Like the droplet of water from the ocean. That single droplet contains all the elements of the ocean, but that little droplet is not the ocean in the ocean's entirety. That single tiny droplet from the ocean is a microcosmic manifestation, a miniature replica of the macrocosm that is the entire ocean. And that tiny droplet can freely move around within the entire ocean. So too, we can freely move around within the cosmic hologram.

The cosmic hologram encompasses each and every reality that is, that ever was and that ever will be, beyond space and time as we know it. That means that absolutely everything in the entirety of creation is contained within the cosmic hologram, and therefore within each and every one of us.  We are each other!

Those who have had a near-death experience all testify to the feeling of complete Oneness, to knowing everything, and to being aware that everything in different levels of reality is all happening in the here and now, all happening currently, yet outside and beyond what we call our normal earthly dimension time flow.

So what we see as events that have happened in the past are actually happening in the here and now! It is only the time frame that governs us here on Planet Earth that makes us see everything is a linear form, as past, present and future.

Reality is simply consciousness manifesting on various energy vibration levels, in different energy dimensions, on varying frequency energy realms. So within the cosmic hologram everything is happening at one and the same time, but on differing energy vibration levels of consciousness. And all the events that we see as history, - they are all happening right here and now!

So the cosmic holographic image and record of all that we see as having happened in the past, is all about differing levels of reality or consciousness. And there are multitudinous levels of reality besides our earth reality. And we can move through these various other levels of reality. That is how psychics operate. They are moving through the cosmic hologram, tuning into other reality levels.

And the famous Dr. Who travelling back in time in his iconic time-machine is indeed nearer the truth than many of us think! The past, or what we consider or perceive as the past, is not gone. It is still out there! It still exists as a photographic imprint on some level of reality. Nothing ends or ceases to exist. Everything just remains in the cosmic store-house, the cosmic hologram, on various levels of reality, on various levels of consciousness.

So if we can travel back in time across the various reality levels in the cosmic hologram and visit other realities, does that mean we can change history?

Definitely not! That football result still stays the same! We are travelling only in an observing capacity! We cannot interfere and save a life or change any outcome.

And travelling through the various reality levels in the cosmic hologram, - this is how we are all multi-dimensional beings, inter-galactic travellers, journeying along the same cosmic highway along which all other levels of reality are also travelling.

**35.** What is eternity? I am a cosmic, inter-dimensional, inter-galactic traveller, travelling throughout all eternity and infinity, beyond time and space. Eternity is not something that begins when I die, when I take my last breath, and then goes on forever. This is it! This is eternity! Here and now!

And each and every life-time, each and every phase of existence, no matter on what energy vibration level I might be, is just another of my countless, timeless walk-abouts across eternity.

Eternity is never-ending. And I as a cosmic, inter-galactic traveller across time and space, will experience all the multitudinous energy vibration dimensions and energy frequency levels in the entirety and eternity of creation.

And so this life-time, in which I am experiencing life embodied in a physical body for the duration of this life-time only, is just another phase, another adventure, another experience all within my soul journey that goes on forever. My eternal soul journey! My soul journey across eternity!

Eternity is the here and now! There is no final frontier. Eternity is on-going, never-ending. This is it!

**36.** There is no such thing as death as we have been gravely (!) misled into believing it to be. To really understand the concept of what we humans call death, and indeed life, we need to remember those 3 words, - ENERGY; VIBRATION; FREQUENCY.

We are all energy. Energy never dies. Energy cannot be killed. Energy never ends. It just transmutes into higher frequencies. Like the caterpillar and the butterfly. The caterpillar does not die. It just transmutes into a different, a higher form.

And so it is with us. We are spiritual beings having a physical experience for the duration of this life-time. And when we come to the end of this physical life-time, we do not end. When we come to the end of our physical life-time we simply discard our physical body, just like an old coat which no longer serves us, or for which we have no further use.

The Hermetic Principle of Polarity or Duality states that everything has what we tend to call an opposite. For example, hot and cold. They appear to be opposites, but really they are just different degrees of the same thing, - in this case, different degrees of temperature. We think of death as being the opposite of life. But again, they are just different degrees, different stages of the same thing, - in this case, the on-going evolutionary journey of each soul.

When we pass over to our next stage of soul evolutionary development, we do not go anywhere in the sense in which we have been led to believe. There is no *place* as such for us to go. There is no heaven, no hell, no purgatory. We simply transmute into a higher frequency level of energy vibration.

As energy, we are all vibrating on a particular energy frequency, depending on how spiritually aware or how spiritually advanced each one of us is. The more spiritually aware we are, then the faster our rate of energy frequency vibration. And the vibration frequency of our energy is the one and only way by which we are ever identified in Spirit.

And the only difference between us and all forms of life throughout all the multitudinous levels of energy vibration frequency in the entirety of creation, is the rate at which the energy of each form of life is vibrating. When we pass back to Spirit, having completed this earthly stage of our soul evolutionary process, our energy vibration speeds up, moves to a faster rate. So our loved ones who have passed on are no longer vibrating on this dense, low earth energy vibration frequency. And that is the reason why we cannot still see them. They are vibrating at a much faster rate than we who continue here on Planet Earth are vibrating. They have not gone away anywhere!

Like the channels on your television or radio. You can only see or hear one of them at a time, - that particular channel you have tuned into. But the others are not gone away anywhere! They are all around you, just waiting for you to tune in!

Like the clothes in your washing machine. As it spins, your physical human eyesight cannot make out any of the items. It is spinning too fast for you to keep up! But when it slows down then you can identify everything, because it has slowed down to a pace with which you can keep up.

Like the propellor of a plane. When it is rotating fast, you cannot see any of the blades, again, because they are going too fast for your human vision to keep up. But when the propellor slows down you can see all the blades.

Like a child's spinning-top. When it is spinning fast, all the colours, all the paintings, all the designs are just a hazy blur. But when it slows down, you can see everything.

So when we pass over back to Spirit, we are simply moving onto a faster rate of energy vibration, higher and faster than the energy vibration we operate on while we are on Planet Earth.

And contrary to what we have also been misled into believing, there is no judgement or punishment to be faced. Judgement, reward or punishment, heaven, hell or purgatory, condemnation to the everlasting fires of hell with no chance of any reprieve, by a despotic god, - none of these actually exist. They are all the invention, the creation, of the Roman Christian Church. All invented to instil fear and guilt into us, in order to exert control over us. Fear and guilt being the most lethal weapons in the mighty arsenal of the Roman Christian Church and other religions. Fear of punishment for sin being the most potent form of deterrent!

The truth is that there is no such thing as sin! Again, sin is the invention , the creation of the Roman Christian Church. Created as a business, a big-time money-making business. A business set up to lure humanity into buying our way into heaven!

We are not sinners! We are bright spiritual beings, having a physical experience for the duration of this life-time, embodied in physical form, in order to fulfil our soul contracts, to learn certain lessons, all in pursuit of our soul expansion.

And there is no such thing as death in the sense in which we have been led to believe it to be. Passing back to Spirit is simply a natural, peaceful transition to another level of energy vibration. There is nothing to be feared. Passing over again to Spirit, to the higher energy vibration levels which are our true home is actually a *'birth'* process. We are being *'born'* again into the Light!

**37.** Religion and spirituality are two very different things! Religion is a man-made set of dogmas, teachings, and beliefs that slot a person into a certain mode of living, into a certain belief system that identifies him as belonging to a particular club. Religion is divisive, controlling, judgemental and punishing. And its chief weapon is fear. Fear and guilt!

Religion promises eternal salvation. And it is a very attractive package. Unfortunately, it does not do what it says on the label! Join our club, pay your money, obey our rules, and here is your ticket into heaven! But what you are really doing is handing over responsibility for your own spiritual development.

Spirituality on the other hand, is none of these. Spirituality is finding one's own way to making a connection with Spirit. Spirituality is recognising and accepting one's own divine essence, one's own divine nature. Spirituality is the acknowledgement and the understanding that you and you alone are responsible for your own soul evolutionary process. Spirituality is understanding that you do not need any intermediaries in order to connect with the One Great Universal Consciousness we call God. Spirituality is understanding that what you seek is already within yourself.

**38.** Connecting with my Higher Self. What is my Higher Self?

My soul is the totality of everything I am, everything I ever have been in any other reality level, and everything I ever will be in any other reality level or energy frequency dimension.

Each time I come into an incarnation, I do not need to take my whole soul with me. I need only a portion in order to fulfil my mission this time around. So I step down only a portion of my soul energy. The rest, the greater part, remains in the **'higher'** levels of energy frequency. And that is what I call my **'Higher Self'**. That part of my soul energy vibration that has not been stepped down. That part of me that is my undiluted God Essence.

My Higher Self, being me in my undiluted God Essence, is omniscient, omnipotent and omnipresent. My Higher Self knows the answer to absolutely each and every question I could ever ask. And my Higher Self, in the purity of the God Essence, will give me all the answers.

And when I pray, it is my own Higher Self, my own divine, undiluted God Essence, with which I am connecting.

**39.** What happens when I pray? Praying is a religious practice, an outward show of faith in a God whom we have been led to believe resides somewhere up beyond the clouds. A God who will grant some of our requests, while withholding others, depending on how long and how hard we pray.

But that God does not actually exist!

When we pray, we are making the connection with our own Divine God Essence, that part of us that is omniscient, omnipotent and omnipresent. Our Higher Self! And it is from our own Divine God Essence that we all get the guidance and the response to our question. Not from an external God, - who does not even exist!

**40.** What is meditation? While praying is an outward religious practice, meditation on the other hand, is an inward spiritual practice.

Meditation is making the connection with our Higher Self or other Beings of Light on other high vibration energy frequency levels.

And it is in moments of silence, quiet, peace and calm that we can most easily make that connection. We cannot connect when we are surrounded by noise and chaos.

When we meditate, we are concentrating on our breathing. Breath is Spirit, Spirit is breath. When we pass over after each life-time, our Spirit leaves our body with our last breath. So breath is Spirit, Spirit is breath. And when we meditate, concentrating on breathing in and out, we very soon reach the stage where we are not just breathing in and out, but we realise we are **being** breathed in and out. And when we get to this point, that is when we have made the deep connection to All THAT IS.

**41.** The Angels and the Higher Beings of Light do not see me as I see myself, a physical being, with certain identifiable features. They recognise only the rate at which my energy is vibrating. And when I pass back to Spirit, the rate at which my soul is vibrating will be the only identifiable or distinguishable feature about me. And my soul will automatically gravitate towards the level of energy vibration frequency in the Spirit world with which my vibration resonates.

It's all about Energy, Vibration, Frequency! Always!

**42.** Mother Nature is my greatest teacher. My guide. My nurse. My provider.

I watch the birds feeding. They take only what they need at any one time. They do not hoard. Simply because they know that when they are again hungry, food will appear. Total trust in the universe to provide.

I watch the flowers turn their heads towards the light. The light makes everything grow, the light gives life to everything.

I watch the river flow towards the open arms of the sea. Everything flows into everything else.

I see the tree standing in the middle of the river. The river does not try to knock it down. It flows around it.

I watch the tides ebb and flow. The rhythm of life in everything.

I watch the moonlight dance on the water. The magic of it all.

I watch the trees bend and sway with the wind. They do not try and stand against the wind, or fight against it. They go with the flow.

I watch the seasons change. Each season has its own beauty. And each season gives way to the next. They each know the time to come and the time to go.

I watch the caterpillar metamorphose into the butterfly. There is no death. Just a  changing into a different form of energy.

Everything I eat, everything I wear has been provided by Mother Nature, Mother Earth.

All the medicines, all the natural remedies and natural herbs are all provided by Mother Nature.

So spend time out in Nature! The greatest show on earth! Sense the elementals as they nourish the soil and the plants. Sense the little water sprites as they tumble down in uninhibited joy over the rocks in the flowing river, or dance on the sparkling waters of the ocean. Sense it all! And nature appeals to all our senses!

The call of nature to us all is strong. Magic lies all around us. And it's all free! Watch closely, listen carefully, and you will see and hear theatrical performances that will dazzle you! And when you make that connection with nature, your life will change. Forever! When you realise that the hand of God is manifest everywhere in nature, you will have found the key to a joyful, peaceful and harmonious life.

So go on, hug that tree! You will both feel the better for it! Let yourself be cocooned in the healing balm of nature, find the magic there amongst the elementals, and they will respond with their love and blessings.

**43.** Karma comes to everyone, without exception. Karma is not a punishment. It is a balancing. A balancing of my not-so-good-deeds with my good deeds. Karma is the internal safety mechanism built into creation. What I do to others, will also be done to me. I get back what I send out. And it might take many life-times for me to balance my karma!

But I do not have to wait that long!

For example, say I send out thoughts of envy to you. What have I just done? I have just sent out a negative, heavy, cumbersome energy. There are no straight lines in nature! Everything is cyclical! And that heavy negative energy I have just sent out is on its way back to be. OUCH!

However, it need not be like this. Energy cannot be killed. I cannot delete what I sent out, I cannot recall it. But I can transmute it! And how do I do that?

I realise what I have done, I regret doing it, and I take responsibility for what I have done. I now send out thoughts of love and light, a high energy frequency, which is travelling much faster than the lower negative energy I sent out previously. And they are both on their way back to me! The higher, faster, lighter vibration will catch up on the lower negative energy, and transmute it! The light always transmutes the darkness!

So when I realise what I have done through my negative, low energy vibration thoughts, and I take responsibility for the toxic fumes I sent out there, I can compensate by sending out high vibration energy thoughts. I can balance my karma!

It's that simple, really!

**44.** There is no point in blaming God when things appear to go wrong. I create my own reality. My thoughts and words draw back to me all that comes into my life. Every thought, every word is a vibration that draws back to me more of the same. I must take responsibility for the thoughts and words I send out!

**45**. EGO means **Editing God Out**. Living in a state of false self. A belief that we can go it alone. A severely limiting belief that it is everyone for himself. A severely limiting belief that we can only experience through our five physical senses. Living in a state of non-alignment with the universal life-flow. When we serve only the false self, we deny the collective human consciousness. We are living in a self-imposed exile.

Living in-Spirit, on the other hand, means we perceive beyond the physical plane to an acceptance, an awareness of other vibrational energy levels with which we are directly and deeply connected. Living in-Spirit engenders our creativity, opens our hearts, making us totally receptive to being **'in-Spired'**, where ideas flow freely as we are connected with Source in the great flow of universal, creative energy.

Living in-Spirit is not a destination we aim to reach, but rather a direction in life that we choose to take, a way of living that we choose to adopt. When we are living in vibrational alignment, in-Spirit, we concentrate entirely on the good and the positive in the world. When we condemn or feel angry with evil doers, terrorists, those who inflict suffering on the world, then we have lost our focus. Living in-Spirit means we accept all the vast diversity of human behaviour and learn from it.

When we live in **EGO**, we are living in the crippling, stifling, limiting world of the self, where we only experience what our limiting five physical senses allow us to experience.

When we live **in-Spirit,** we experience the freedom of the vastness of the greater whole, - an **'inspired'** life of unlimited potential, beyond our mere physical senses.

**46.** The man in the mirror. I cannot change anyone else's energy. I can only change my own energy. I am not responsible for what anyone else does. I am only responsible for myself. When I change my own energy, then I attract like energy to me.

So if I want to change the world, I start with the man in the mirror. I change my own energy vibration frequency and then everything else will change too.

One person at a time!  Starting with the man in the mirror.

*'Im starting with the man in the mirror,*

*I'm asking him to change his ways,*

*And no message could have been any clearer*

*If you wanna make the world a better place,*

*Take a look at yourself, and then make a change.'*

**47.** A rainbow is not just a beautiful arc of colours in the sky, to be admired. Colour is a vibration. That means it sends out an energy frequency. There are 7 colours in the rainbow. There are seven chakras in the human body, all of different colours, and all the same colours as the colours of the rainbow.

All energy vibrations attract the same back to themselves. Hence, when I watch a rainbow, my chakras are attracting the vibrations of the colours. My base chakra attracts the red of the rainbow, my throat chakra attracts the blue of the rainbow, my solar plexus attracts the yellow and so on. So I am receiving a charge of energy through my entire chakra system.

And you thought a rainbow was just a beautiful display of colours in the sky, to be admired?

**48.** Everything flows in a natural rhythm. The tide flows in, the tide flows out. We come and we go through all eternity, just changing energy form. There is a measured, controlled motion in absolutely everything. The pendulum swings to the right and then to the left to the same degree. Nothing lasts. The good times don't last, and neither do the bad times. And how do we apply this in our everyday lives? By treasuring and appreciating the good times when we have them, being grateful for everything because we know the good times will not last. And then when times are difficult, knowing that this too will not last.

**49.** Creating a new world. We need tools, not weapons!

Hermann Goering, chief of the Nazi police state said at his trial, when questioned, that it was **fear** that enabled the Nazis to get so much control. Fear! The most lethal weapon in any arsenal!

And what weapons do we have to counteract fear? We have no weapons. We do not want weapons. We do not need weapons. And why not? Because we have tools. And tools are very different from weapons!

Weapons are destructive. They destroy, they kill, they maim, they tear asunder. Tools, on the other hand are constructive. They build, they repair, they fix, they put together again.

And we have the two greatest tools that could ever be envisioned at our disposal. We just do not understand or realise the power we have with these two tools. And what are these two tools? These two tools are Love and Light! And with Love and Light we are constructing a beautiful new world, built on solid foundations.

War cannot be fought with more war. Violence cannot be met with more violence. Anger cannot be met with more anger. No problem can ever be solved if we remain on the same low vibrational frequency level on which the problem has manifested. We must raise our energy vibration to a higher level of frequency and consider it all from that higher vantage point.

**50.** Casting pebbles. We stand on the shore, at the water's edge and cast a pebble into the water. Why? What is the attraction? - To see the effect our pebble has on the vast ocean! To see our little pebble start a ripple effect that goes on and on. And we stand and watch, fascinated.

Never underestimate the power of the ripples you create! Those ripples you create in your daily life by just a smile, a caring word, a helping hand. You never know the effect a smile, a kind compassionate look, a gentle squeeze of the hand, can have on anyone.

When you feel someone is having a bad day, give them a gift. It does not always have to be something material. How about a hug? A smile? A compliment? Good wishes? A pleasant greeting? Then just watch as a miracle unfolds before your very eyes! Just watch as a great ripple starts to spread from you to them and then out beyond them to everyone else they meet! What you have just done here is, you have raised their vibration by making them happy, and they are in turn raising the vibration of others.

Make someone happy, and then you will be happy too! That's because you have sent out that high vibration energy frequency, which must, by the inviolable Spiritual Law of the Universe, come back to you, multiplied!

That's the ripple effect! That's how it works!

Mother Teresa said:

*'I alone can't change the world, but I can cast a stone across the waters to create many ripples'.*

So cast your pebbles! And know that as you cast, you are initiating the ripple effect! And you will never know where that will end! Or whose life you will affect for the better!

**51.** Crystal, Rainbow and Star Children are living amongst us now in ever- increasing numbers. These high vibrational souls require high vibrational parents to help them throughout this life-time. They have come here at this particular time, from higher vibrational realities, to help in the raising of the earth's vibration, by simply spreading love to all those around them. They have no other agenda apart from raising our earth's energy vibration level and they are doing just that in the only way in which it can be done, - spreading unconditional love.

**52.** Unconditional love does not mean being in denial about anyone else's weaknesses or negative traits. Nobody is perfect. If we were, we would not need to be here in this dense earth vibration level of reality. Unconditional love is seeing beyond those negative traits to the beautiful, spiritual beings we all are, here to fulfil soul contracts. We are all simply playing a part on the stage of life.

**53**. Trust in the Universe. When you throw babies up in the air, they laugh and gurgle, because they know you will catch them again. That is trust!

The universe knows what you need and want, and the universe delivers!

Just trust!

**54.** There is no such thing as an absolute of anything. We tend to see hot as being the opposite of cold. But in reality they are just different degrees of the same thing, - in this case, temperature. The same with death and life. They are not separate states. They are both part of the same journey of the evolution of a human. Everything is the same yet different at the same time. For example, look at a photograph of yourself when you were younger. Are you now the same or are you different? You are BOTH the same person, yet also different. Or the newly painted fence. Is it the same fence or is it different? It is BOTH the same fence and yet also different. And how do we apply this in our everyday lives? By being aware that there is no such thing as an absolute of anything. Everything **IS** and **IS NOT** at the same time. Everything needs to be balanced!

**55.** There is neither a right way nor a wrong way to do anything. There are only  different ways. We are all on the same journey. We are just taking different routes. Some are taking the straight route. Some are taking the scenic route. But we will all  get there in the end.

**56.** Healing can only happen when the energy frequency is raised above that of the problem. Violence, war, hatred, greed, - these are all low energy vibration frequencies and they all create problems. They all upset the natural flow of universal energy.

We need to raise our vibration above the level on which the problem is manifested. We need to move up to the vibration of Light and Love.

In the words of Martin Luther King:

*'Returning violence for violence multiplies violence, adding deeper darkness to a night already devoid of stars. Darkness cannot drive out darkness; only the light can do that. Hate cannot drive out hate; only love can do that.'*

**57**. I am always in the right place at the right time. There is no such thing as chance, coincidence or luck! There is only synchronicity. Synchronicity is the coming together in the universe of all the elements needed to manifest a particular outcome.

Everything is in order. Everything is as it should be.

**58.** That which I criticise in others, I see in myself. The universe is a mirror, reflecting everything back to us.

**59.** The hero within each of us! There is only the one story, - the rise of the hero within each of us! All the fairy tales, all the great novels, - they are all about the rise of the hero, each one of us facing our demons, our weaknesses, overcoming obstacles, learning lessons, to make us stronger, to progress on our spiritual evolutionary path.

**60.** Life's but a game! And with every game, there are rules. And it is only when we understand the rules, - then we are able to play the game! To play the game of life and win!

**61.** The truth will always be revealed. Of this we can be certain. It may take some time, but the truth will always come out!

**62.** Where intention goes, energy flows. Where you place your desires, your intentions, then your thoughts send out an energy frequency that attracts what you wish back to you.

**63**. I create my own soul song. I have a unique song, a unique note to contribute to the One Great Cosmic Orchestra. No one else can sing my song, and I can sing no one else's song.

**64.** It's all about the journey. It's not about getting to the destination. We have all eternity to do that. It's about the experiences along the way. The experiences that make us grow and evolve our soul.  So take your time! Smell the roses! Just be!  Just be in the here and now, in this present moment!

**65.** Be like the eagle. The eagle soars high above everything, seeing the whole picture. Be like the eagle. Do not get bogged down in small, trivial matters. Look at the whole picture. Stay in your high energy vibration level! Stay above this dense earth vibration energy level!

**66.** Cause and Effect. Every cause has its effect and every effect has its cause. There is no such thing as chance happenings or coincidence. There is only synchronicity. And how do we apply this in our everyday lives? By being aware that by changing our vibration, we can change both the cause and the effect. We are in control with the thoughts we send out!

We can change our vibration. And the *'effect'* of changing our vibration is that it sets in motion a whole new chain of events. We can *'cause'* things to happen by the thoughts we send out. We can manipulate the *'effects'*.

**67**. My soul knows where to go when I leave this earth energy frequency dimension. It has made this journey many times before. I will automatically gravitate towards my Monad, my soul family, and the vibration frequency with which my soul is resonating.

**68.** Everything has both a male and a female element. There must be a balance between the female energy and the male energy in both ourselves and in our world. And how do we apply this on our everyday lives? By understanding that the male and female energies are not in competition. Rather, they complement each other. The two make up the whole.

**69.** The whole universe is but a vibration, in constant motion and movement. The only difference between us all is the vibratory rate of our energy, - the rate, the speed at which our soul, our energy is vibrating. That is how we are recognisable throughout the entire energy frequency vibration network. That is how we are identified! And how do we apply this in our everyday lives? By keeping our vibration high, by understanding that like energy attracts like, - by taking back our power through understanding that everything, absolutely everything is vibration, and by sending out only high energy vibration thoughts and words.

**70.** Everything comes from the same Source, the Great One Universal Mind, and is drip-fed, filtered down through all the different energy vibration frequency levels, with constant inter-action, constant inter-communication, between all the levels. And how do we apply this law in our everyday lives? By being open to receive! Being open to being IN-SPIRED! IN-SPIRIT! Being receptive!

**71.** Everything originates in the One Great Universal Mind, the One Great Universal Energy, the One Great Universal Consciousness we call God. *'The All is Mind'* as the *'Kybalion'* teaches us. All energy and matter at all levels is created by, and is subordinate to the omnipresent One Great Universal Mind. Our mind is part of the One Great Universal Mind, the only difference between any of us being the level of degree of our reality. And how do we apply this law in our everyday lives? By accepting that our thoughts create our reality and by taking responsibility for those thoughts!

**72.** The 3-plumed flame of yellow, blue and pink. Symbolic of the 3-plumed flame of knowledge, power and love. Yellow is for knowledge; blue is for power and pink is for love. The 3-plumed flame spirals upwards, all 3 colours balanced with each other, simultaneously dancing, intermingling in a synchronised movement of light and colour, no one colour dominating over any other. All in perfect balance and harmony.

And that is exactly how knowledge, power and love should be in balance.

Knowledge is like money, - it is use-less if it is not spread around, if it is not kept in circulation, if it is kept to oneself. Money in itself has absolutely no value. Its value lies in what it can buy, as a medium of exchange. Knowledge too must be circulated to have any value.

Power without love is mis-use of power. Power without love is controlling, manipulating, domineering, suppressing.

Love too must be spread around. *'Spread your light for everyone to see!'* Don't hide it under a bushel. The world needs love, to help raise us all to a higher vibration level. The basis of everything is love. Love is synonymous with God. God is love. Love governs all things.

Knowledge without love is dead. Knowledge without the power to spread it around is really only wasted information. Power without love is only manipulation for certain ends and control.

Knowledge, power and love must all be in balance in our lives.

**73.** A Sioux Indian Prayer:

*'O, Great Spirit whose voice I hear in the winds, and whose breath gives life to all the world, hear me. I am small and weak. I need your strength and wisdom.*

*Let me walk in beauty, and make my eyes ever behold the red and purple sunset.*

*Make my hands respect the things I have made and my ears sharp to hear your voice.*

*Make me wise so that I may understand the things you have taught my people.*

*Let me learn the lessons you have hidden in every leaf and rock.*

*I seek strength, not to be greater than my brother, but to fight my greatest enemy - myself.*

*Make me always ready to come to you with clean hands and straight eyes.*

*So when life fades, as the fading sunset, my spirit may come to you without shame.'*

**74.** This Great Awakening. 2021 is the year of our great awakening. If everything was going peacefully, we would all just drift along, asking no questions, just passively accepting, accepting, accepting. It is when times get tough, when things become disturbing, when we cannot understand or see the logic in what is happening around us, - then and only then do we start to ask questions. And that is good! All this craziness around us now, all this lack of logic, all this propaganda, - all is serving as a wake-up call to all of us!

A wake-up call to become more aware, to start thinking for ourselves, to take back responsibility from those who have abused and misused our trust.

As Hitler said:

*'How fortunate for governments that people do not think!'*

**75.** Overcoming superstition and ignorance - man's greatest challenge. Ignorance and superstition are man's greatest enemies! Inherent in ignorance and superstition are prejudice and fear. All toxic, negative energy! And humanity continues to be trapped in the swirling vortex.

Superstition is based on ignorance, ignorance of the truth. As is prejudice. As is fear. Fear is the greatest over-riding negative energy in our world, the polarity, the opposite to love.

**76** It's a wonderful world. See your glass as neither half empty **nor** half full, but as overflowing! We always have free will. We can choose to see these present times  as all doom and gloom, nearing another Armageddon. Or, we can choose to see them as  a wonderful opportunity to get back in touch with our inner self,  to find once again what we seem to have lost somewhere along the way.

Never, ever, focus on the negative. Always on the positive. Remember, what we focus on, we draw into our lives. We attract illness to ourselves if we send out fearful thoughts of becoming ill. If we think or talk poverty, we will experience poverty. If we think or talk wealth, we will experience wealth.

So focus on the beauty all around you, on the abundance of Mother Nature, on the good of everyone, and send out love and blessings to all, to the entire universe.

Because remember, in the midst of all the hardships, it is still a wonderful world!

**77.** Native Indian 10 Commandments:-

1. The Earth is our Mother, care for her

2. Honour all your relations

3. Open your heart and soul to the Great Spirit

4. All life is sacred, treat all beings with respect

5. Take from the Earth what is needed and nothing more

6. Do what needs to be done for the good of all

7. Give constant thanks to the Great Spirit for every day.

8. Speak the truth but only of the good of others

9. Follow the rhythms of nature, rise and retire with the sun

10. Enjoy life's journey, but leave no tracks

**78.** We must work from the heart and not from the head.  We must become aware of our free will to make various choices. We must also become aware of the consequences or effects of our actions. We must become aware of whether our actions will bring happiness or unhappiness to ourselves and to others. And where can we find direction and guidance as to what choice to make? In the heart! Not in the head! Only your heart can tell you what is best for you to do. We need to bring ourselves out of the mind and into the heart. The heart is holistic and intuitive, unlike the head, which is conditioned by so many influences.

Follow your heart and become a conscious choice-maker!

**79.** When we live in the here and now, when we are fully experiencing the present, when we are aware of everything around us, when we are living every minute, we are living in the Oneness. And when we are living in the Oneness, we are experiencing being part of it, and so we will know without any doubt whatsoever that whatever we desire is available to us whenever we want it. And why? Simply because when we are living in Oneness, we are living in joy, peace, and happiness, and any desire we have is sent out to the universe from that place of contentment and joy, knowing it will be delivered, and not from the level of fear, anxiety or desperation.

**80.** Being grateful. Show gratitude for everything you have got. Focus on what you have, and not on what you do not have. When you express gratitude, you set in motion a whole energy vibration that brings more of the same back to you.

When you pay your bills, do not do so grudgingly, or with resentment, as that creates a blockage in the flow of positive energy. Bless your bills as you pay them, thanking the universe for providing you with the money to pay them, and showing your heartfelt appreciation for the services you have enjoyed, thereby increasing the flow of positive energy.

*Thank you, Universe for all the gifts and blessings you are constantly sending me! I am open to receive more.*

**81.** Taking responsibility. We have an awesome responsibility! We have the awesome responsibility for the thoughts we send out. Each and every thought, emotion, word and action of each and everyone of us , - they all send out an energy frequency vibration that attracts similar energy, and manifests.

We are all encompassed in the One Great Universal Energy we call God.  There is no separation. We are all an inherent part of, and not apart from, the One Great Universal God Energy.  So we are co-creators within that all-encompassing Divine Oneness. We are the great Universal God Energy experiencing itself.

Where our intention goes, energy flows. When we focus our attention on something, that is what we materialise.

We are co-creators! We have created everything in our world by focusing our attention on it. Poverty, disease, hatred, prejudice, corruption, greed, violence, war, religious fanaticism, abuse of power, - these are all distorted mutations of the ALL THAT IS, human miscreations that we have materialised through our human ego.

But no matter how dark or contaminated our human miscreations are, the energy within the core of that miscreation still pulsates with its original divine potential. This is true for every person, place, condition, or thing existing on this planet. For instance, in the core of every expression of poverty still pulsates the divine potential of infinite abundance, and in the core of every facet of disease still pulsates the divine potential of vibrant health.

It is when we focus on illness and disease rather than on health, on war rather than on peace, on poverty rather than on plenty,  that we empower and sustain these negative aspects in our lives. It is just that simple. Through our lack of understanding we have created a vicious circle for ourselves. With the limited perception of our fearful human ego, we end up focusing our attention on the surfacing patterns of for example, poverty, instead of on the patterns of infinite abundance.

**82.** Choosing my crystals! So you think you choose your crystals? Actually, the crystals choose you! A particular crystal in the shop resonates with your energy and you feel a pull towards it! It's crying out to you:

*'Over here! Over here! Buy me! Buy me!'*

And when you run your hand over the stones, you will feel a pull towards a particular stone. That's the one you will take home with you!

And you cannot choose a crystal for anyone else. You can certainly buy a crystal for someone, but that person must be in the shop with you, in order for the crystal to connect with that person's energy. That's because it is the crystal that does the choosing.

Fill your home with the beautiful energy of crystals. Programme your crystals to bring peace and joy to all who enter your house.

And don't forget to cleanse and re-charge them all in the moonlight!

**83.** Living with joy is our natural birth right. Life is not meant to be a struggle. It is we ourselves who create the struggle when we constantly push against the flow of Divine Ordinance, when we are not connected. Just do whatever it is that makes you happy. The happiness and joy you get from just doing what you love doing, permeates your entire body, spreading out into your auric field and then out to everyone you meet. The reason why you came here in the first place was to raise your own vibration, your spiritual awareness, and the collective consciousness of all humanity. How easy is that, when all you have to do is just something you love doing! Couldn't be easier! What is there not to be happy about?

**84.** The universe operates and functions through giving and receiving. The flow must be kept in dynamic continuous movement. This is an abundant universe, with enough for everyone, but all must be kept flowing, in circulation. Whatever we stop flowing or circulating, we stop its circulation or flow back into our own lives. Whatever we hoard, we will lose. Money, like everything else, must be kept in circulation. Otherwise, it has no value.

The more you give, the more you receive in return, and not necessarily from the same person. The more you keep the flow going, the more will come back to you. When you give from your heart, with unconditional love, not asking or expecting in return, you set in motion an unstoppable flow of energy that must, by divine law, bring a return to you, multiplied many times.

Keep the circuit open. If only two people are involved in the process, you are actually closing the circuit. Keep the circuit open by giving to as many different people as you can. Better to give a little to a number of people than to give a lot to the same person all the time. Give widely, with love, expecting nothing in return, and just watch as the universe increases its flow of all good things back to you.

And be open to receive! To receive all the gifts and blessings nature bestows on us all constantly. And to receive from other people. Every soul cries out to give, and when we do not allow ourselves to receive from someone else, then we are denying that person the right to score spiritual brownie points. Whether it is a kind compliment, a helping hand, a listening ear, a piece of advice, a present, - whatever, - receive with joy and gratitude.

We must learn to both give and to receive, all in balance, to maintain the flow.

**85.** Music of the Spheres. All the planets in movement, as they rotate, create a melody of sound, - a vibration, a perfect harmonious note that resonates throughout the entirety of creation. There is a *'Song of Planets',* a *'Cosmic Hum'* to be clearly heard! And that musical vibration of all the planets affects us here on earth. Our quality of life here on earth is indeed influenced by this vibration of the planets and the universe.

Music is a vibrational gateway, a gateway into a higher, expanded state of consciousness. As we become One with the music, we then become One with the Great Universal God Energy, the Great Universal Consciousness.

**86.** The earth is a living organism. Each one of us is a microcosm of the macrocosm of that living organism. We have lungs to enable us to breathe. The trees are the lungs of the earth. We have an immune system to keep us safe from disease and illness. The earth has an immune system, - the vast biodiversity and eco systems that sustain healthy life.

Lock-downs, social distancing, wearing of masks, hand washing, - these are all the methods our present governments have implemented in order to solve this present world health crisis.

But these methods are only treating the symptoms, not the cause of the problem, not the dis-ease itself!

And what is the cause? What is the dis-ease? The cause of our problem is the devastation of earth's biodiversity and eco systems, the very systems that are in place to protect us! And we wonder why we are in a pandemic!

We need to change our attitude to Mother Nature! We need to decrease our consumerism! To end our exploitation of earth's natural resources! We have plundered, we have depleted, we have ravaged Mother Earth! And we wonder about all these, what we call 'natural disasters'! Mother Earth is crying out to us for attention! Mother Earth is suffering! Gasping for breath!

But in the midst of all the devastation we are causing, we have three great things working in our favour.

First, we as humanity can change. And we can change quickly! We have shown that over the last year! Our governments are doing u-turns every day! We have changed our habits completely, - work, socialising, school, shopping, funerals, weddings. This time last year if you went into a bank wearing a mask, you would have been arrested and taken away in handcuffs! And now? You can't get in without one! Yes! We can change, - and quickly!

Secondly, these lock-downs are actually working in our favour. They are buying time for Mother Nature to recuperate.

And thirdly, Mother Nature and all our biodiversity and eco systems are self-replenishing, self-sustaining, self-healing. They do not need us to help them replenish. They just need us to stop devastating them!

The problem however is that we are depleting and devastating more rapidly than they can recover! It takes only a few minutes to chop down a tree. But it takes years for a tree to grow again. A whole forest can be cut down in a short space of time, but it takes years and years to grow again.

So you see, we are the problem!

A healthy eco system means healthy soil, means healthy plants, means healthy food, means healthy people.

Ecology must come before economy, and not the other way around, as we have been doing!

We need to change our attitude to Mother Nature. We need to change our relationship with the animal kingdoms. And we need to cop ourselves on to the damage we ourselves are doing to our eco systems, - the very systems that are the immune systems of the earth!

**87.** Humanity needs to return to living from the heart. Your heart is your mechanism, your channel, your conduit, through which you receive and transmit divine Love and Light. Your emotions, your feelings, your sexuality all come from and through your heart. Those same inherent feelings and emotions which are the great signposts, the great informers, the great guides on the journey of your soul.

You have been living like a computer, - programmed for everything you do. But you are not a computer. A computer has no heart. A computer cannot feel or show emotions. Those who would control you know the power of emotions and the great power that emotions generate. Generated and organised emotions can topple governments and all sorts of institutions. That's why you have been taught to deny and suppress your feelings and emotions.

Your emotions are divine aspects of yourself, states of pure feeling, generated from within yourself. And anything coming from within yourself does not lie, manipulate or deceive you.

However, often you confuse your emotions with judgements, when you feel shame, guilt, anger or whatever. These are not true feelings, true feelings coming from your heart, for your heart in its pure form knows only truth, unconditional love and compassion. Truth, unconditional love and compassion come from Source, so your heart always leads you back to Source.

Everything changes constantly in you except the beat of your heart. Listen to your heart! Live from your heart! Open your heart! Follow your heart and live a truly fulfilled life!

**88.** Your body is a beautiful manifestation of the creativity of the One Great Universal Energy. A beautiful manifestation of Father/Mother God. You need to love and nurture your body. Loving your body means loving being you, being happy in your own skin. Loving yourself means seeing yourself as the bright spiritual being and light you really are. Loving yourself means not judging yourself, not harbouring feelings of guilt, not beating yourself up over something you have or have not done. Loving yourself means accepting yourself exactly as you are, here and now. All that is on the surface is false. The beauty lies beneath. It is the soul light that shines out, and it is that soul light shining out that gives beauty and radiance to the body.

**89.** We are only passing through on this earthly plane, only travellers on our long walk-about across the infinity of eternity. This earth plane is simply a bridge between dimensions, and when we see it as such, we do not get attached to what this world offers us, because we see everything as temporary and passing. Life goes on in a continuous flow, constantly changing, and it is our resistance to impermanence that causes us most of our pain and suffering. The dimensions beyond this earth dimension are those on which we need to keep focused, as they are the reality, this dimension being only temporary and transitory.

**90.** There is an ancient Hawaiian Mantra that has been used by the Kahuna, the mystic healers, for centuries. It is very beautiful. It is called **'HO'OPONOPONO'.**

Just close your eyes and imagine anyone or any situation where you are having difficulty or experiencing trouble. Repeat these four simple phrases, with honest intention:

**I AM SORRY**

**PLEASE FORGIVE ME**

**I LOVE YOU**

**THANK YOU**

**91.** We are not alone in the Universe. We are only one of a multitudinous number of civilisations, all vibrating on different energy frequencies and dimensions. many of them millions of light years ahead of us. There are other life forms out there, all greatly advanced from us in technology. We here on Planet Earth are not the sole living organisms in a limitless and boundless cosmos.

Our Planet Earth is not the centre of the universe! And the reality is that our little world is just that - little, - in the vastness of the entirety of space.

We are not from Planet Earth. We have been seeded by beings from other planets. And we will not be allowed to destroy this Planet Earth! We are being watched and monitored. For our own good! For our own safety! To protect us from ourselves!

Our brothers in space are out there! And maybe it is time for us to meet them!

Is a visitation imminent?

**92.** You have the power! The power of your thoughts! The power of your thoughts to create your reality. The power to change famine and starvation into plenty for everyone. To end war and bring peace to every place on earth. To rid the world of fear and fill it with love.

Use your power wisely! Use it well! Envisage! Envisage! Envisage! Use your magical powers to create a magical world for everyone! You are magic in action!

You can do it! Go for it!

**93.** Our young people are our hope for the future! We must equip them with the proper tools to enable them to do their job of salvaging what they can from this present chaos. A chaos not of their making!

We must teach our young children the spiritual laws of the universe.

We must show our young people the damage our consumer society is doing to the earth's support systems, the very same support systems on which we depend for our very existence.

**94.** Namaste!  The God in me recognises the God in you.

*I honour the place in You*

*Where the entire Universe dwells.*

*I honour the place in You*

*Which is of Love*

*Of Truth*

*Of Light*

*And Of Peace*

*When you are in that place in You*

*And I am in that place in Me*

*We are One.*

**95.** I am light

I am truth

I am Divine Essence

I am the Divine made manifest

I am abundance

I am eternal love

I am the breath of Life

I am one with the Source

I am perfect design

I am Peace

I am divine will

I am unconditional Love

I am that I am that I am

**96.** Atonement. - At-ONE-MENT.

At-One-Ment means letting go of the world of fear and returning to the world of love, leaving the world of separation and returning to the world of wholeness. It means living in the vastness and the greatness of the wholeness, in the magnificence of our true identity rather than struggling in the limited identity of the small body or ego. It is the getting rid of the illusion of death, sin and loss and coming into our own natural state of harmony and peace, in the Oneness that is All.

**97**. *'Whoever has self-knowledge, the world cannot contain them'.*

*'Those who know the All, yet do not know themselves are deprived of everything'.*

The words of Yeshua in the Gospel of Thomas.

Self-knowledge is a consciousness, an awareness of the energy which each one of us is, and our connection to all the other countless vibration energy frequencies which surround us on all sides, constantly inter-communicating, inter-penetrating, inter-being with us and with each other.

'KNOW THYSELF!'

**98**. We cannot buy happiness, good health or inner peace, no matter how much wealth we are able to accumulate, no matter how many material possessions we are able to gather. Happiness cannot come from transitory material possessions. Wanting less, being satisfied with what you already have, and taking time to appreciate and enjoy it all is a major key to happiness and inner peace.

**99.** Give your home a good clear-out! De-cluttering your house is de-cluttering your mind. Feel the weight fall from your shoulders! The weight of being weighed down with too much material possessions. We are spiritual beings, and when we pass back to Spirit after this life-time, to our next stage of existence, we will take no material possessions with us.

**100.** Let your light shine! You have come from the Light and it is to the Light that you will return. You are unique! You are one of a kind! You are of the great God essence, shimmering in your splendour! Sparkling in your magnificence! Awesome in your greatness! Unlimited in your potential!

You are beautiful! There is only the one you! You have a unique job to do while you are here on Planet Earth. No one else can do your job, in just the same way as you cannot do anyone else's job either. The job you yourself chose for you to do before you entered your present incarnation.

In your daily life, shine your light for everyone to see. When those who live in darkness, in the absence of the light, see your shining light, they are drawn to you like the moth to the flame. They are drawn to realise that there is somewhere else for them to exist rather than in the debilitating darkness where they now find themselves. And it is your bright, shining sacred light of your soul that will light up the path for them. It is your bright, shining sacred soul-light that will rescue them from the misery of existence in darkness.

*'This little light of mine, I'm going to let it shine!........Let it shine! Let it shine! Let it shine!'*

# Other Books by Eileen McCourt

Eileen has written 32 other books, including her first audio-book which has recently been published. All are available on Amazon. For more information, visit her author page:

www.eileenmccourt.co.uk

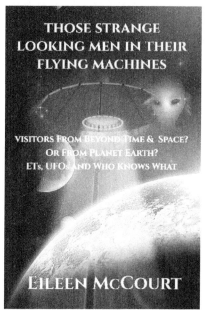

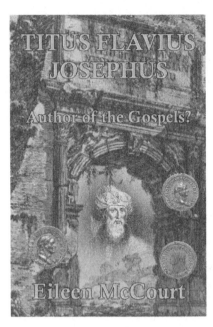

Audiobook

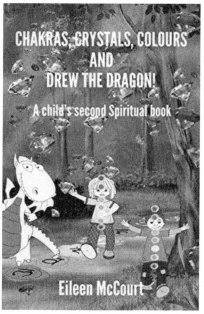

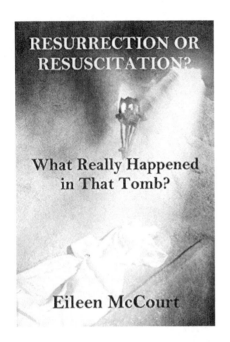

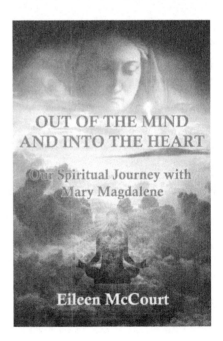

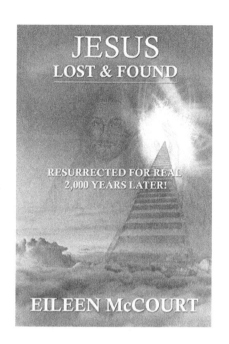

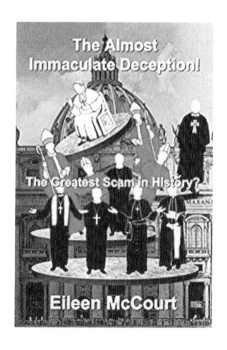
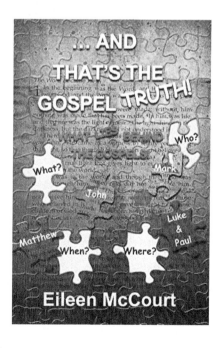

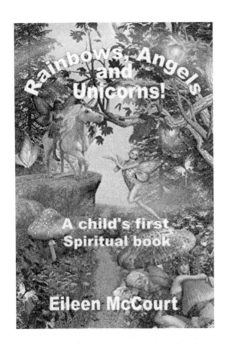
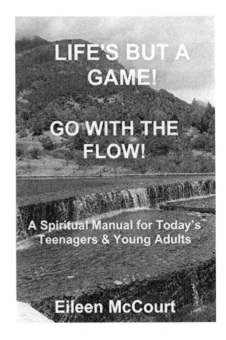

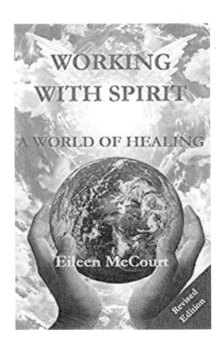

150

Printed in Great Britain
by Amazon